SHAQ!
THAT MAGICAL ROOKIE SEASON

The Orlando Sentinel

Orlando, Florida

TRIBUNE
PUBLISHING

Orlando, Florida / 1993

SHAQ!
That Magical Rookie Season

This book was made possible by the
extraordinary day-to-day and game-by-game
coverage of Shaquille O'Neal and the Orlando
Magic during the 1992-93 basketball season
by the photographers and reporters of
The Orlando Sentinel.

EDITOR / BILL DUNN

ART DIRECTOR / MARK A. WILLIAMS

CHIEF PHOTOGRAPHER / GARY BOGDON

TEXT / TIM POVTAK, KENNETH AMOS

ELECTRONIC IMAGING / GEORGE REMAINE

PHOTO RESEARCH / BOBBY COKER

Copyright 1993
Tribune Publishing
Photographs and text copyright 1993
by *The Orlando Sentinel*

TRIBUNE PUBLISHING

EDITORIAL DIRECTOR / GEORGE C. BIGGERS III

MANAGING EDITOR / DIXIE KASPER

SENIOR EDITORS / BRUCE CARDEN, KATHLEEN M. KIELY

PRODUCTION MANAGER / KEN PASKMAN

For more information about this and other books from
Tribune Publishing, contact:

Tribune Publishing
P.O. Box 1100
Orlando, Florida 32802-1100

(407) 420-5680

FIRST EDITION

Library of Congress
Cataloging-in-Publication Data
Shaq! : that magical rookie season / the Orlando sentinel
        p.   cm.
    ISBN 1-56943-014-4. -- ISBN 0-941263-91-6 (pbk.)
    1. O'Neal, Shaquille.   2. Basketball players – United
    States – Biography.   3. Orlando Magic (Basketball
    team)   I. Orlando sentinel.

GV884 . 054S43   1993
796 . 323'092--dc20   93-8364
[B]   CIP

Cover photograph: Gary Bogdon

I've got a lot to learn, but one day,
I'm going to be the man in this league.
You can write that down and underline it three times.

February 7, 1993, America West Arena, Phoenix, Arizona: Shaquille O'Neal 1, Backboard 0. With a power slam, the rookie brought the goal standard to its knees, causing a 37-minute delay in a nationally televised game. After the incident, the NBA strongly advised all teams to have a serviceable spare ready to roll in the future.

"A goal shall be made when the ball is thrown or batted from the grounds into the basket and stays there . . . "

Dr. James Naismith, meet Shaquille O'Neal.

Man-child.

Megarookie.

Baby Monster.

The Real Deal.

His tomahawk slam dunks may not be exactly what you had in mind when you spelled out the original rules and played the first basketball game using two peach baskets. But in 1993, more than 100 years after you invented the game, the 7-foot-1, 300-pound rookie center of the NBA Orlando Magic was taking the world of professional basketball by storm with dunk after rim-rattling dunk. Undoubtedly, they would have turned your peach baskets into toothpicks.

We think you might have enjoyed watching this remarkable story unfold as much as we did.

SHAQ!
THAT MAGICAL ROOKIE SEASON

Edited by Bill Dunn

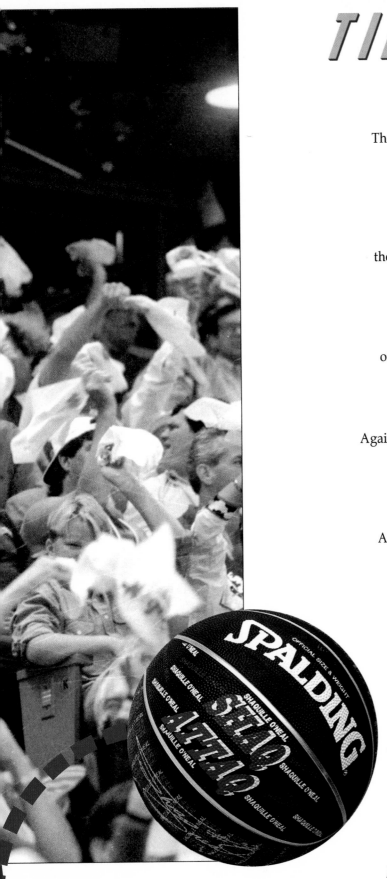

TIME TO PLAY

CENTER OF

ATTENTION

With unprecedented hoopla for a rookie in any sport, Shaquille O'Neal fired the imagination of the American public . . . and it was only the beginning

By Tim Povtak

t began innocently enough with a bent rim and a big smile on the first day of training camp. That was playful power. It ended on the final week of the season with a smashed basket support in East Rutherford, New Jersey, and people running for cover. That was pure business.

The dunk became his signature. The Shaq Attaq.

In between, Shaquille O'Neal of the Orlando Magic left an indelible stamp on the National Basketball Association with the most celebrated rookie season in the history of professional sports.

The Herculean force of his game, the impact of his presence and the furor he created were astounding.

He arrived with enormous expectations – the No. 1 pick in the college draft, the largest contract in league history and the weight of a franchise resting on his shoulders.

He disappointed no one. He was bigger, better and wiser than anyone had imagined. He was everything advertised and more.

It wasn't just what he did – finishing among the league leaders in points, rebounding, blocked shots and field goal percentage – but how he did it that left everyone so fascinated with his feats.

He was power with playfulness. He was so mature, yet so innocent at times, lost in his youthful exuberance and unaware of what he had created. He was serious, yet he wanted to be outrageous. He was a millionaire, but he fed the homeless. He was a man watching the world through a youngster's eyes. He was a refreshing contradiction, and people loved it.

His rookie season was like a

Tim Povtak is a sportswriter for The Orlando Sentinel *assigned to cover the Orlando Magic.*

1

trip through wonderland, a story-book ride down Fifth Avenue in a ticker-tape parade. The basketball schedule became his parade route. And every day became a Fourth of July celebration for Shaquille O'Neal.

People clamored to see him at every stop. They waited for hours in hotel lobbies, outside arenas, often circling the court during pregame warmups. They wanted a closer look, a chance to yell his name, maybe to catch his attention.

The Magic, a team that previously traveled in virtual anonymity, suddenly became second only to the Chicago Bulls in road attendance. Only Michael Jordan was a bigger attraction in the NBA.

"It was fun, a lot of fun," the rookie said when it finished. "It was great being me. I saw a lot. I learned a lot. And I think I held up pretty well. Next season I'll come back improved."

At 7-foot-1, 300 pounds, he was physically unprece-dented. In the history of sport, there never has been anyone this big who was this quick

His high school won the Texas state championship in 1989 with a 36-0 record, then saluted his contribution by retiring his jersey.

Basketball wannabes of all shapes and sizes have matched up for years during pick-up games at the Fort Sam Houston Sports Arena. Shaquille was one whose dreams came true. "There was no doubt he was going to be a big-time player," said Cole High School Coach Dave Madura. "But he never flaunted it. He was probably the most popular kid in the school."

and this athletic. He made it clear from the start: He aspired to greatness. He had that on-court desire to dominate. And he had the tools to achieve his goals.

He was the season's first Player of the Week, the first time a rookie had ever won the award at the start of the season. He was Rookie of the Month for four consecutive months. Fans elected him as the starting center on the Eastern Conference All-Star team, the first rookie to start in the game since Jordan in 1985.

In a final kudos that surprised nobody, he was named NBA Rookie of the Year.

More than once, he grabbed a defensive rebound, dribbled up court and he dunked at the other end.

Shaquille did it all in this magical rookie season.

At a time when the NBA needed another marquee player – following the retirement of Magic Johnson and Larry Bird – Shaquille O'Neal came along.

"The league needs someone like Shaquille," Jordan said. "It was time for someone like him to come along. We welcome him with open arms. He is someone else who can help carry this league."

Shaquille didn't shy from the attention. He often bathed in it. When the bright lights of television went on, he lit up. The first time the Magic appeared on network television – against Phoenix in February – he broke his first basket support, pulled it right down with a thunderous dunk. The game was delayed for 37 minutes, and the legend grew. He mugged for cameras. He looked for microphones. He was the

youngest player in the league (he turned 21 on March 6), but also its most intriguing. The infectious, crooked smile and the charismatic manner made him attractive to

Cole High School yearbook photo, 1989.

almost everyone. He loved the game, and he projected well into the crowd. He winked. He waved. He pointed, making eye contact with those sitting courtside and above.

"I'm not an actor, but I am an entertainer," he said. "I'm paid a lot of money to do what I do, so I want people to enjoy watching me play. I'd like to be like Michael Jordan, and go into any arena in the country and have the people cheer. I want to give them their money's worth."

There were no hoots and hollers on the road, only oohs and aaahs. They gasped at his strength, even when he beat the home team. They cheered him in Jersey when he beat the Nets. They applauded in Chicago when he beat the Bulls. They clapped even in Boston when he beat the

Celtics.

Although he was paid like a king ($40 million, seven years,) to play basketball, he was paid even more to lend his name and time to corporate America. Companies that sold shoes, soft drinks, toys, sporting goods, trading cards, all competed to earn his endorsement before his first season had ended. Some started before his first season had begun.

"He's part Bambi and part Terminator," said his business agent Leonard Armato. "I don't know if there's ever been anyone like this before. It's like Disney managing Mickey Mouse. Everyone wants to link Mickey with their product. Same way with Shaq."

Already worth millions, the prime-time rookie took time out of the limelight to remember the needy. On Thanksgiving, he held a "Shaqsgiving dinner" at a homeless shelter in Central Florida, where he served more than 300 people. At Christmas, he played "Santa Shaq," and brought toys to more than 1,000 needy children. When he saw the poor sleeping conditions at the shelter, he bought the homeless new beds.

On Valentine's Day, he bought a rose for every patient at a hospital in Orlando. When he heard about a runaway truck that had plowed into a school bus stop – killing one child and injuring a half-dozen more – he asked for directions to the hospital. More than once, when he saw a poor person with a sign "WILL WORK FOR FOOD," standing along a road, he stopped and took that person to lunch.

"I'm so fortunate that sometimes I can't believe it," he

Comparing Shaquille O'Neal's NBA rookie season with other great rookie centers

YEAR	PLAYER	GP	FG%	FT%	REB	BLK	PTS AVG
1956-57	**Bill Russell**, Boston	48	.427	.492	19.6	NA	14.7
1959-60	**Wilt Chamberlain**, Philadelphia	72	.461	.582	27.0	NA	37.8
1969-70	**Lew Alcindor**, Milwaukee	82	.518	.653	14.5	NA	28.8
1974-75	**Bill Walton**, Portland	35	.513	.686	12.6	2.7	12.8
1984-85	**Hakeem Olajuwon**, Houston	82	.538	.613	11.9	2.7	20.6
1985-86	**Patrick Ewing**, New York	50	.474	.739	9.0	2.1	20.0
1989-90	**David Robinson**, San Antonio	82	.531	.732	12.0	3.9	24.3
1992-93	**Shaquille O'Neal**, Orlando	81	.562	.592	13.9	3.5	23.4

said. "I just hate to see others suffer. That kills me sometimes. I have the money to help, so why not. I wake up every morning and thank God that this is my life."

During a travel day late in the season, he made a morning appearance at a Stay in School program at an Orlando middle school, but he turned it into a very special event.

Instead of the perfunctory few words that players normally give, he donned his rap outfit, brought along teammate Dennis Scott and performed a song-and-dance routine that had the assembly room shaking. He also brought along $100 bills to distribute to the students who had earned the Most Improved Student, Best Citizen

and Hardest Working awards. They were stunned.

"If I was going to do it [attend the assembly], I wanted to get the kids' attention. You can't do that with a speech. They don't listen all the time," he explained later. "It wasn't that big a deal. We had fun. They enjoyed it, and I think we got our point across."

He loved to make people

laugh, telling jokes, playing jokes. Collecting hats became a hobby during the season. He would arrive with a different one each game, each becoming a little more comical. First there was a black leather one that looked like something the confederates wore in the Civil War. Then came a foot-tall black top hat like Lincoln might have worn.

Shaquille's mother, Lucille, in a quiet moment with her son after a Magic loss to lowly regarded Dallas.

"I wanted all my children to have unique names. To me, just having a name that means something makes you special."

– Lucille Harrison

(In Islamic tradition, Shaquille Rashaun means "Little Warrior.")

Then there was an equally tall red-and-white striped hat from *The Cat In the Hat*, and the black-and-white striped one like the Mad Hatter's. He loved being noticed, being recognized, being outrageous.

He told everyone at the NBA All-Star Game in Salt Lake City that he wanted to go flying down a snowcapped mountain on an inner tube. He told them that when he returned to Orlando, he was going bungee jumping. He is the same guy who first stepped off the plane in Orlando wearing a pair of Mickey Mouse ears.

On his first trip to New York as a pro basketball player, he unveiled a full-length leather coat with a big "S" on the back. He often left Orlando Arena, after games and practice, in his customized Ford Explorer with "Shaq Attaq" plates and a sound system that would work well in an open-air stadium. The rap music he played was heard two blocks away as he smiled and drove off.

Early in the season, he would finish practice, then put on his music and entertain coaches and teammates with his break dancing skills, dropping to the floor and spinning on his back like a giant top. After baskets, he might do his "ninja strut," stalking down court with stiff arms and legs, bulging mouth and wide-open eyes.

At one point during the season, he traveled with a jheri-curl wig that sometimes allowed him to walk past autograph seek-

Shaquille's father, Philip Harrison, and nephew, Malcolm, 4, absorbed in some March Madness.

ers without being noticed. But that rarely worked. Normally, he was mobbed at every stop.

But through all of his foolishness, his basketball ability was the reason people laughed and looked and cared so much about him. He opened the season with an 18-rebound performance against the Miami Heat, the most rebounds for a rookie in a first game since Bill Walton in 1974. "When he leaned on me, it was like a house falling on you," said Miami center Rony Seikaly.

At the end of his first week, he had 21 rebounds in a victory against Washington, outrebounding the entire Bullets starting lineup.

O'Neal struggled with foul trouble and free-throws early, but he improved as the season progressed. His passing improved too, which was imperative because of all the double-teaming and collapsing defenses he faced. The Magic finished the first month of the Shaq era with an 8-3 record, the best month in franchise history.

From there, he was well-marked by opponents and well-known throughout the country. He also was involved early in a mini-controversy. His coaches felt the officials were calling too many fouls against him. Opponents said he was getting too many breaks for a rookie. But all that passed.

Before the season was finished, he had appeared on the cover of *The New York Times*

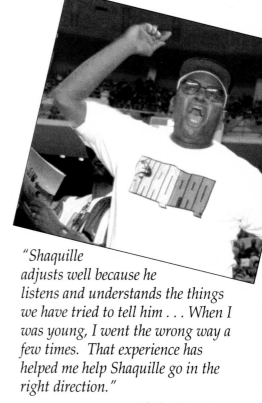

"Shaquille adjusts well because he listens and understands the things we have tried to tell him . . . When I was young, I went the wrong way a few times. That experience has helped me help Shaquille go in the right direction."

– Philip Harrison

PRO SCOUTS LOVED LSU'S 'MAN-CHILD' SHAQUILLE

Long before he announced his availability for the pro draft – after his junior year at LSU – basketball scouts were raving about Shaquille. He combined all the skills anyone could want in a big man: scoring, rebounding, shot-blocking, intensity at both ends of the court.

They spoke of the 19-year-old junior in terms of his "man-child" body, and his great, quick feet, and the rocket-like spring in his legs, a quality rare in a person his size.

In his college performances, the scouts saw the quickness of David Robinson, the strength of Patrick Ewing and the agility of Hakeem Olajuwon.

One scouting report referred to him as "a 7-foot Charles Barkley."

Said Orlando Magic General Manager Pat Williams, who then could only speculate about what such a player might mean to his expansion franchise: "He's a warrior. There's a kind of noble quality about him. He is special beyond his basketball abilities. He's going to be one of the special ones that this league thrives on, a marquee attraction who's going to make a team very good."

At the time, Williams could only wish that the Orlando Magic would be that team.

But a lot can happen when you wish upon a star.

Magazine, Sports Illustrated, Sport, TV Guide, Ebony and a variety of other publications. On the Magic's first trip to the West Coast, he appeared on *The Arsenio Hall Show*, performing his rap act with the band Fu Schnickens. Music was his release from basketball.

He and the band also performed at the Stay In School Jam at All-Star Weekend in Salt Lake City.

As the season progressed, he tired at times, but it hardly showed. People waited for him to hit The Wall, that mythical barrier that most rookies encounter in their first grueling NBA season, but he never did. He knocked it down, instead.

He finished the season among the NBA leaders in a variety of categories: ninth in scoring (23.4 per game); second in rebounding (13.9 per game); second in blocked shots (3.53 per game); and fourth in field goal percentage (.562). He was the first rookie since Buck Williams (1981-82) to have both 1,000 rebounds and 1,000 points in a season.

His highs included 46 points against the Detroit Pistons, 24 rebounds against the Chicago Bulls, nine blocked shots against the New York Knicks and six assists against Washington. His lows included 7 points against Detroit on and 9 turnovers against Philadelphia. He finished with a team-record 307 turnovers.

Although he failed to propel the Magic into the NBA playoffs, they improved from 21 victories in 1992 to 41 victories in 1993, the most improvement of any NBA team. He had been everything the Magic could ask for.

"There are a lot of great players in this league, but I don't think I'm there yet," he said. "Someday, I'm going to be The Man, the top guy. The day will come, believe me . . . This was just the start."

From top: Shaquille embraces family members at LSU; devours sandwich as sister Ayesha jokes about his appetite in an April 1992 photo; enjoys the sweetness of victory with Tiger teammates.

...THE

*T*he luckiest day in the history of the Orlando Magic led to the easiest decision they ever would make. The luck involved winning the draft lottery – when that Ping-Pong ball with the Magic logo popped out of the hopper. That gave them the right to select first in June 1992 at the NBA college draft.

So convinced Shaquille would be the NBA's next superstar – and so eager for him to begin work – the Magic quickly signed him to a seven-year, $40 million contract, the most lucrative in league history. It was easily the richest for a first-year player in

any sport, and the earliest signing of a No. 1 pick since the NBA's salary cap was instituted in 1983. The negotiations went surprisingly quickly. But the parameters were simple.

His agent asked for the biggest contract in basketball history. The Magic agreed. Their biggest problem was making room under the salary cap, which meant renegotiating contracts with five other Magic players. Once that was done, the deal was signed.

The celebration officially began. And it all started with a little bit of luck.

1992 NBA Lottery Draft

		Player	Pos	Ht	College
1	Orlando	Shaquille O'Neal	C	7-1	LSU
2	Charlotte	Alonzo Mourning	C	6-10	Georgetown
3	Minnesota	Christian Laettner	F	6-11	Duke
4	Dallas	Jimmy Jackson	G	6-6	Ohio State
5	Denver	LaPhonso Ellis	F	6-8	Notre Dame
6	Washington	Tom Gugliotta	F	6-10	N.C. State
7	Sacramento	Walt Williams	G/F	6-8	Maryland
8	Milwaukee	Todd Day	G	6-8	Arkansas
9	Philadelphia	C. Weatherspoon	F	6-7	So. Mississippi
10	Atlanta	Adam Keefe	F	6-9	Stanford
11	Houston	Robert Horry	F	6-9	Alabama

FIRST PICK

... ORLANDO

The city best known for Mickey Mouse adopted Shaq as its newest favorite son

$40,000,000.00

Contract-signing day brought a smile to everyone's face, from those getting the money, to those giving the money. Clockwise from O'Neal are Pat Williams (Magic general manager), Leonard Armato (Shaquille's agent), Dick DeVos (Magic president) and Rich DeVos (Magic owner).

GOES GA GA

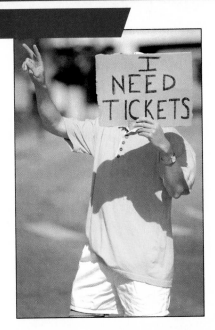

Shaquille's appeal was so broad in Central Florida that the bus company used him to promote its mass-transportation efforts. By putting his likeness on a bus, officials said they increased ridership, especially among the younger crowd. The bus was unveiled in February, just after O'Neal was named the starting center for the Eastern Conference in the NBA All-Star Game.

RAW...

Even a veteran coaching staff could not hide the amazement at some of the things it saw in the first close-up look at Shaquille. Although training camp at Stetson University in DeLand lasted only five days, the rims on all of the baskets in the gymnasium had been bent from the force of Shaquille's powerful dunks. The Magic happily paid to replace each one. Camp was designed around Shaquille, helping him make the transition from college to professional basketball. His muscles were sore from the two-a-day practices, but not as sore as the players who tried to guard him. It wasn't a matter of a rookie trying to fit into the system, but trying to design a system to best fit the rookie.

*B*efore training camp had finished, everyone knew how special the prized rookie really was. He snagged rebounds, then turned and drove the ball up court. He outran some of the guards during speed drills. He was out-muscling everyone around the basket.

More than once – after a thunderous Shaquille dunk – veteran center Greg Kite looked upward toward the ceiling, wondering if the whole gym was coming down around him. "I've been around this league a long time," said veteran center Mark McNamara, who was brought in specifically to work with Shaquille. "And I've never seen anyone with this kind of potential."

The Magic focused on integrating Shaquille into the system, and learning exactly how everyone could fit in around him.

When the staff met each evening to discuss the progress that day, nobody ever bothered trying to hide his excitement. All of them knew what was coming.

The league's next superstar was just getting started.

SHOWTIME!

They were amazing, electrifying, spellbinding, daring and explosive — and those were just the halftime acts

nd now-w-w-w-w-w-w, ladies and gentlemen, stand and che-e-e-r, your-r-r-r- Orlando-o-o-o-o-o-o-o-o Magic! (CUE PYROTECHNICS.)

Win or lose, game nights in the Orlando Arena with Shaq and Knuckleheads were always a mix of athleticism and Barnum & Bailey. The widest range imaginable of *Star-Spangled Banner* renditions, followed by fireworks and hyperextended player intros:

"Tom Tol-l-l-l-l-l-l—bert."

"Great Scott-ott-ott-ott-ott."

"Nick An-n-n-n-n-n-nderson."

"Scott Sk-i-i—i-i-i-iles."

"Shaqui-i-i-i-i-i-i-i-i-i-l-l-e O'N-e-e-e-e-e-e-al."

There were magicians and dancing girls. Disco, rap, rock 'n' roll and backpack basketball. Celebrities and laser lights and . . .

"Two-o-o-o-o-o-o for Bo-o-o-o-o-wi-e-e-e."

"Magic nuts! Get your Magic Nuts!"

"Cinnamon roasted al-l-l-l-l-l-l-monds!"

. . . and, that other nut, STUFF.

The guy with the blue hair. The guy with the Superman signs. And The Fat Guy.

The Toyota Time Trials. The Dodge Dash for Cash. The Subway Sub of the Game. The Mac Attack!!!!!

Then, too (DRUM ROLL, PLEASE): the wondrous and incredible Pelligrini Brothers! . . . the amazing and amusing Quiddlers! . . . the delightful and fantastic Vita Family! . . . the gravity-defying and spellbinding Alexis Brothers . . . the electrifying and devilishly daring Bud Light Daredevils! . . . and explosive Alison Bly, the Dynamite Lady!

All things considered, a Magic home game made for quite an evening out.

As it all ended, and you were headed home, you almost expected to hear the announcer remind you that, yes, Elvis had left the building.

Day-o!

Day-ay-ay-o!

At times, Coach Matt Guokas looked a little like a maestro trying to conduct a rap band.

FIRST GAME—FIRST WEEK

S haquille didn't ease into his first NBA season. There was no rookie orientation or any period of adjustment. He arrived in full bloom, bigger and brighter than all of the hoopla surrounding him.

After four games, he was picked NBA Player of the Week, the first time in league history any rookie had ever won the award at the start of a season. Michael couldn't do it. Larry and Magic never did it. Patrick couldn't do it either.

Shaquille just did it.

He had 18 rebounds on opening night at Orlando Arena, helping the Magic beat rival Miami. He had 22 points and 15 rebounds the next night in Washington, leading the Magic to victory over the Bullets. The kid was for real, and everyone knew it. At 20, he was the youngest player in the league, but

FIRST GAME	Magic 110, Heat 100						
player	min	fg-a	ft-fta	reb o-t	a	f	tp
O'Neal	32	4-8	4-7	5-18	2	6	12

he immediately was one of the best.

He had 35 points the third night. In those three games, he had 10 blocked shots. He was no seed in need of nurturing, like most rookies. He arrived as a giant sycamore, forcing others to adjust to his imposing presence. The Magic had found the man to build their championship hopes upon.

Word spread quickly around the league. It was double-team the rookie or risk having him embarrass you. Suddenly, opponents thought twice about driving the lane against the Magic, something they had done automatically in the past.

In the fourth game, again against Washington's Pervis Ellison, one of the league's better young centers, Shaquille had 31 points, 21 rebounds and 4 blocked shots. The season had begun with a flourish.

The Magic had changed forever.

Shaq on the sideline? Oh, no! Oh, yes! That's just where opponents wanted the rookie. But he spent only about 10 minutes per game there, much of it after getting into foul trouble. Except for some scratches and bruises, and occasional lower back pain, Shaquille played his rookie season free of injury.

Against Hakeem Olajuwon *(Houston Rockets, two games)*

O'Neal	14.0 points per game	15.0 rebounds per game	2.5 blocks per game
Olajuwon	21.0 points per game	14.0 rebounds per game	4.5 blocks per game

Defensively intimidating? He can be, and in a variety of ways.

Opponents tried a myriad of ways to stop Shaquille. None worked consistently. They played him to the left, to the right, from the front and the back. It started with one defender and soon became two, and sometimes three, once he touched the ball. The Detroit Pistons even tried the "Foul Him" defense, preferring to give him free throws instead of dunks. As the season progressed, the rookie began learning the tricks, making the right passes to make teams pay for overplaying him.

Against Patrick Ewing *(New York Knicks, four games)*

O'Neal	21 points per game	14.5 rebounds per game	4.75 blocks per game
Ewing	15 points per game	13 rebounds per game	2.25 blocks per game

Against David Robinson *(San Antonio Spurs, two games)*

O'Neal	17.0 points per game	13.0 rebounds per game	2.5 blocks per game
Robinson	26.5 points per game	11.5 rebounds per game	2.0 blocks per game

One aspect of his game in need of improvement – he missed 294 of 721 free throws.

Against Alonzo Mourning *(Charlotte Hornets, two games)*

O'Neal	29.0 points per game	12.5 rebounds per game	3.5 blocks per game
Mourning	24.0 points per game	11.0 rebounds per game	1.0 blocks per game

For someone Shaquille's size (7-1, 300 pounds), his athleticism was unprecedented. No one this big in the NBA had ever been this quick or agile. He could outmuscle the big men, then outrun the smaller men. He said that if not for basketball, he probably would have become a dancer. As a youngster, he practiced break dancing with his friends. After Magic practices, he sometimes provided his teammates and coaches a glimpse of those skills. Occasionally, as in the sequence that begins on the previous page and continues here, a game would become a test of gymnastics.

Against Robert Parish *(Boston Celtics, five games)*

O'Neal   22.8 points per game   14.2 rebounds per game   2.6 blocks per game

Parish   16.6 points per game   9.0 rebounds per game   1.4 blocks per game

Against Brad Daugherty (Cleveland Cavaliers, four games)

O'Neal	22.5 points per game	13.3 rebounds per game	2.0 blocks per game
Daugherty	19.0 points per game	10.7 rebounds per game	1.3 blocks per game

It might be just a matter of perspective

Although Shaquille's rookie season was filled with fanfare, it also had its controversy over the way game officials treated him.

Both he and the Magic coaching staff believed that officials often penalized him – made calls against him that they didn't make against other superstars. He fouled out of eight games. Foul trouble followed him throughout the season. He was ejected twice. He committed a team-record 307 turnovers.

"Rookie calls," is the way he often described it. Opponents many times felt just the opposite – that he was getting star treatment from the officials because

the league loved his notoriety. When Magic Coach Matt Guokas called the league office to complain about the treatment, he was told there was an opposing coach on the other line with the opposite view.

No one had ever seen anyone so big move so fast, which may have caught officials as well as opponents by surprise. Rookies traditionally don't get the benefit of the doubt. O'Neal did at times. But often he did not.

"I guess it just depends on which side of the fence you're standing on," said Rod Thorn, the NBA's director of operations. "You have to remember, Shaquille is unique."

Shaq and Spud form a web of body parts as Goliath is challenged by David up the middle.

Against Rony Seikaly *(Miami Heat, four games)*

O'Neal	18.2 points per game	15.0 rebounds per game	3.0 blocks per game
Seikaly	14.0 points per game	7.0 rebounds per game	.3 blocks per game

INC.

$$$$ $$ $$$$$ $$$$$$ $$$ $$$$ $$ $$$$$$$ $$$ ... $$$$ $
$$$$ $$ $$$$$ $$$$$$ $$$ $$$$ $$ $$$$$$$ $$$$ ... '$$$ $$

*T*he Orlando Magic aren't the only ones hitching their hopes on Shaquille. The business world has made it quite fashionable, too.

His man-child image – a basketball giant with the playfulness of a kid – created an immediate competition for his endorsement signature. It assured him a salary that exceeded his basketball earnings.

Even before he signed with the Magic, he had signed a shoe contract with Reebok (five years, $20 million) and a card contract with Classic Cards (two years, $2.5 million). Then came deals with Spalding (four years, $6 million), Pepsi (five years, $10 million), and Kenner Toys (three years, $1 million). This is only the beginning.

No athlete in history has capitalized so quickly upon entering professional sports. Not only was his contract with the Magic (seven years, $40 million) the most lucrative in the NBA, his endorsement earnings immediately put him second in the league behind only Michael Jordan.

Shaquille's endorsement contracts are unique in that all of them are linked by the *Shaq Attaq* logo that is showing up everywhere today. It's a plan that Shaquille's agent Armato designed and the various companies have accepted as part of the deal.

Shaq isn't just the hottest player in the NBA. He's the hottest thing in the marketing world, too.

Shaquille with his "elders" (Bill Russell, center, and Bill Walton) during Reebok taping; and, below, announcing the Spalding deal.

Before Shaquille signed with Orlando, some marketing gurus warned that from an endorsement standpoint, he would be better off in L.A. But, the Magic drafted him and the choice was no longer his. Looking back, it's hard to imagine this lovable baby monster accomplishing more commercially than he did from Orlando – collector cards, soft drinks, shoes, apparel, toys, videos, video games. What's next? Music, movies, more books, comic books? And who knows what else. Reebok's president Paul Fireman put it best: "Obviously he's a one-man PR company."

LOVE
Sha**q**! $16.00

$16.00

$13.00

Orlando
Magic

SH★QUILLE 32
o'neal

$5.00

$12.00

ORLANDO MAGIC
FANATTIC
SPORTS CENTER

GAME NIGHT SPECIAL

Delong Satin Jackets

Quilted Black
and White
$84.00

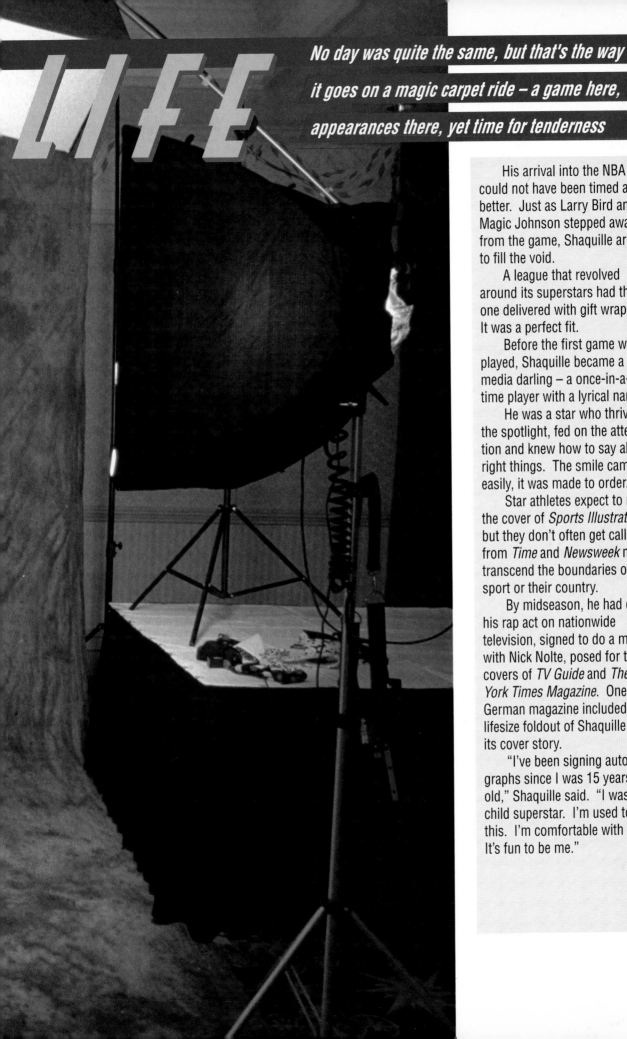

LIFE

No day was quite the same, but that's the way it goes on a magic carpet ride — a game here, appearances there, yet time for tenderness

His arrival into the NBA could not have been timed any better. Just as Larry Bird and Magic Johnson stepped away from the game, Shaquille arrived to fill the void.

A league that revolved around its superstars had this one delivered with gift wrapping. It was a perfect fit.

Before the first game was played, Shaquille became a media darling — a once-in-a-life-time player with a lyrical name.

He was a star who thrived in the spotlight, fed on the attention and knew how to say all the right things. The smile came so easily, it was made to order.

Star athletes expect to make the cover of *Sports Illustrated*, but they don't often get calls from *Time* and *Newsweek* nor transcend the boundaries of sport or their country.

By midseason, he had done his rap act on nationwide television, signed to do a movie with Nick Nolte, posed for the covers of *TV Guide* and *The New York Times Magazine*. One German magazine included a lifesize foldout of Shaquille with its cover story.

"I've been signing autographs since I was 15 years old," Shaquille said. "I was a child superstar. I'm used to all this. I'm comfortable with it. It's fun to be me."

SUPER
SNEAKS
CONTEST

The impact and influence of the rookie superstar stretched far beyond the basketball court where he makes his living. He reached out and touched his community in a fundamental fashion. He joined in local events such as the annual Black Tie and Tennies Charity Gala, benefiting the Orlando Magic Youth Foundation recipients, above. He fed and visited the homeless on Thanksgiving. In a Santa cap, he donated toys at The Salvation Army and other Orlando area community centers. At Christmas, he swept through a toy store one night purchasing toys to pass out to disadvantaged children.

Shaquille tries his hand with some virtual reality gear, gunning down some bad dudes.

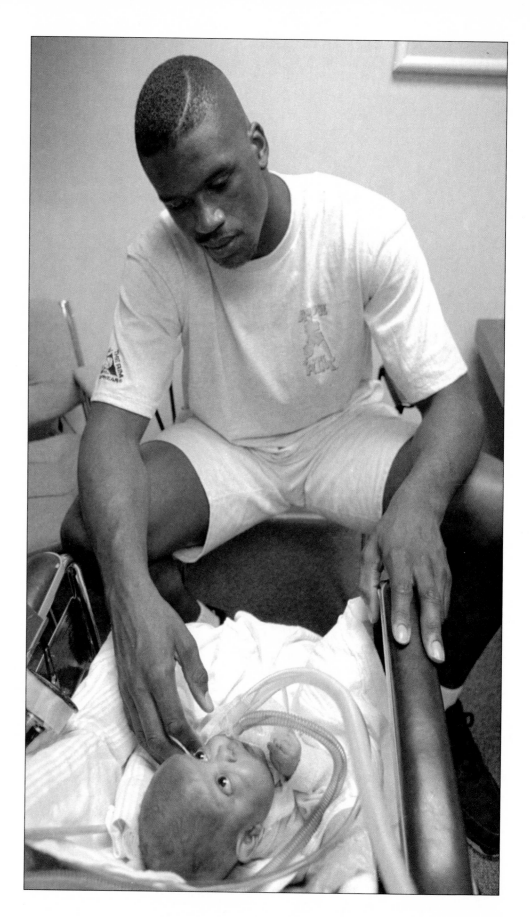

Elijah seemed a bit timid at first when the big man walked into his hospital room bearing gifts for his first birthday party. Elijah was born with chronic lung disease and had spent his entire life at the hospital.

A future star in the
making? Shaquille
starts 'em young –
and short – at the
blacktop basketball
clinics he conducts.

Dear Shaq:

I am a big fan of yours. I watch you a lot because I used to like the Mavericks, but they are terrible this year. I also saw Inside Stuff when you dunked and the rim came off. Cool.

John, **age 12, Dallas.**

The mail started coming before he even arrived. By midseason, it became a daily avalanche into the offices of the Orlando Magic. The staff mail cart was replaced by a mail truck. On the slow days, there were 150 pieces. On the busy days, it topped 400. People wrote to say thanks, to offer advice, to ask for tickets, time or money, and to tell him that they named their children and, once, a pet iguana, after him.

At right and below: Shaq's shack, a spacious $720,000 Cape Cod style mansion located in well-heeled Isleworth.

Teammates compared traveling with Shaquille to traveling with a rock star, watching him tapdance through crowds at every stop. His celebrity status made normal travel impossible. To avoid the commotion that he would cause by walking through large airports and traveling on commercial flights, the Magic traveled on their own plane. It was a luxury that made life easier for everyone. There was plenty of leg room for the players as they stretched out on customized lounge chairs and sofas. Hotel lobbies were particularly interesting as crowds always gathered just for a glimpse. The rookie tried various disguises, using dark glasses, outrageous wigs and hats. But nothing really worked, forcing him to exit hotels by going down the stairwells and outside doors to the waiting bus.

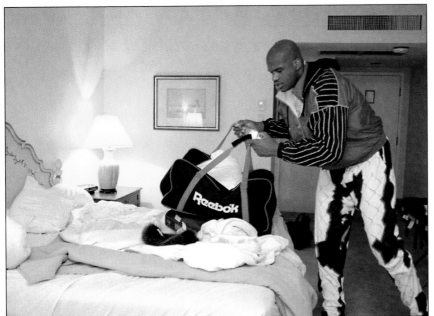

No two days were exactly alike during his whirlwind rookie season. There was a time to work, but always a time to play. A time for kids (and the game-night ritual with a different "Shaq Paq"), and for kidding around, and for magic moments: the kudos from boyhood hero Julius Erving, and yes, opposite page, some Ninja garb shenanigans with the press, after a surprisingly easy win over the Miami Heat.

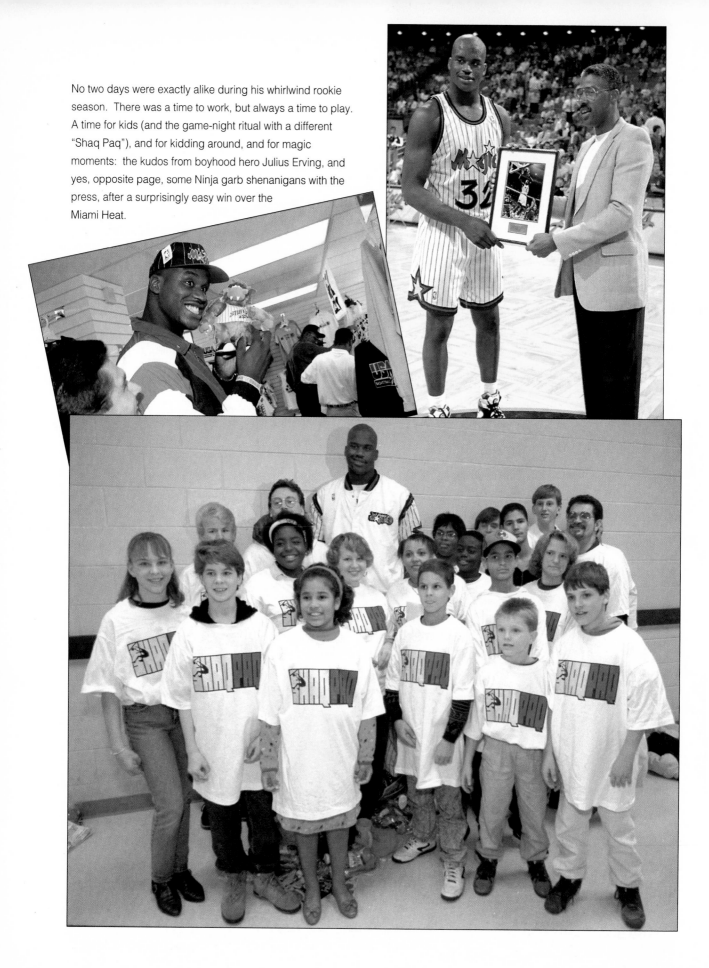

ALL-STAR

When the All-Star votes were counted, the rookie rated fourth overall, and started over Patrick Ewing at center

1951	1954	1957	1960	1961	1962	196
			 MVP	 MVP		
Bob Cousy BOSTON	**Ray Felix** BALTIMORE	**Tom Heinsohn** BOSTON	**Wilt Chamberlain** PHILADELPHIA	**Oscar Robertson** CINCINNATI	**Walt Bellamy** CHICAGO	**Jerry Lu** CINCINN

is name was spelled wrong – O'Neil – on the NBA's original All-Star ballot, but the 826,767 fans across the country who voted him into the starting lineup knew exactly who he was.

All-Star Weekend was the official coronation for the league's newest superstar.

Shaquille became the first rookie since Michael Jordan in 1985 to start in the NBA's showcase event. But not even Jordan had come into the game with such fanfare.

O'Neal arrived in Salt Lake City on Friday for All-Star Weekend with an entourage that included his agent, his personal assistant and four members of the Orlando Magic staff.

"Maybe next time, I'll have my own plane to bring everyone in," he joked.

He was engulfed by autograph seekers upon his arrival, and they followed him everywhere. Although his weekend was tightly booked – with media interviews, corporate hand shaking and

965	1966	1969	1980	1982	1985	1992

Jackson	Rick Barry	Elvin Hayes	Magic Johnson	Isiah Thomas	Michael Jordan	Shaquille O'Neal
ADELPHIA	SAN FRANCISCO	SAN DIEGO	LOS ANGELES	DETROIT	CHICAGO	ORLANDO

> *He's going to be one of those guys that after you play him, you sleep real good.*
>
> – Magic Johnson, *television analyst*

official NBA functions – he enjoyed the experience thoroughly.

He spent some time with Paula Abdul. He played some one-on-one basketball with Isiah Thomas. He clowned with Charles Barkley. He sat with the veterans and helped judge the Slam Dunk Contest.

He sang "What's Up Doc?" during his performance with the rap group Fu Schnickens at the league's Stay in School Jam. It was the first time any All-Star player had ever performed a musical act at the festivities. In more ways than one, he was unique.

His All-Star jersey was sold for a record $55,000 during a charity auction, $30,000 more than Michael Jordan's jersey. The fans in Salt Lake City couldn't get enough of him.

The ovation he received before the game was the loudest for anyone other than home-town favorites John Stockton and Karl Malone of the Utah Jazz. When he acknowledged the fans, they cheered even louder.

He started and played 25 minutes for the Eastern Conference. He made a thunderous dunk that shook the basket support. He showed enough that everyone knew he would become a regular at this annual event.

He had 14 points and seven rebounds. His performance, though, was secondary to his being there. He brushed aside a mini-controversy over his playing time. This was too good a weekend to spoil with pettiness.

"It felt great being Shaquille O'Neal this weekend," he said. "And hopefully, the fans will ask me back."

Upset over playing time? Shaquille, the diplomat, replies

Fans voted Shaquille the starting center for the East team in the 43rd annual NBA All-Star Game, but coach Pat Riley had the final say on another front. He controlled who played the most. Riley kept him on the bench for a 16-minute stretch in the second half, using him for just 25 minutes in the West's 135-132 overtime victory. Riley, coach of the New York Knicks, used Knicks' center Patrick Ewing for 25 minutes, too, often playing him at power forward alongside Shaquille. The rookie was diplomatic when asked about Riley's rationing of the playing time. "No, I wasn't upset, I was just glad to be out there having fun." Riley earlier had told reporters that NBA fans should have voted Ewing the starting center. He later said his comments had been taken out of context. Shaquille, the first rookie to start in the game since Michael Jordan in 1985, made 4-of-9 field-goal attempts and 6-of-9 free throws.

Patrick Ewing on Shaquille: "He's a great player. He plays hard and is very strong. He knows how to find people when he needs help in the post. He is going to be a great pro."

Top ten All-Star ballots

1	Michael Jordan	1,035,824
2	Scottie Pippen	932,912
3	Charles Barkley	858,947
4	Shaquille O'Neal	826,767
5	Clyde Drexler	823,482
6	David Robinson	803,696
7	Larry Johnson	658,236
8	Patrick Ewing	578,368
9	Karl Malone	563,627
10	Chris Mullin	515,779

MORE THAN A FOOT

You are looking at Shaq's sneak's actual size. What size? Here are the answers to this and other curiosities about professional basketball's newest main man.

Shirt size: 52
Waist: 46
Hand size: See page 72
Shoe size: 20 EEE; Actual size below

Vertical leap: 36 inches
Body fat: 10 percent

Contract: Seven years, $40 million

Birthday: March 6, 1972

Mother's height: 6-2
Father's height: 6-7
Height in junior high: 6-4
Height as a high school sophomore: 6-8

Number of brothers and sisters: 5

Boyhood hero: Julius Erving

Best subject in high school: Geometry
Worst subject: Government
Nickname at Cole High School: "Shock"
O'Neal, Shaquille "The Deal" O'Neal
Cole High superlative: Nicest smile
(Joe Cavallero was chosen "Most athletic")

First car: '89 Dodge Dynasty
Current car: Burgundy Ford Explorer

Favorite toy then: Stretchable Hulk figures
Favorite toy now: Speakers in his truck

Number worn then: 33
Number worn now: 32

College sophomore points per game: 27.6
College junior points per game: 24.1

Favorite food: Macaroni and cheese
Favorite pizza: Cheese
Favorite sub: Turkey

Average pieces of fan mail received per day: 250

Main off-court interests: rap music, karate
movies, arcade games, acting

Favorite rap group: Fu Schnickens
Favorite TV cartoon character: Shazam
Favorite Disney character: Aladdin
Favorite dance: Break dancing
Favorite movie: Anything with kung fu fighting

Favorite animal: Doberman pinscher

If he weren't a basketball player, he'd probably be:
a rapper, disc jockey, actor or comedian

Square footage of home: 7,000

Favorite NBA city to visit: East Rutherford, N.J.
Least favorite NBA city to visit: Milwaukee

Shaquille's picture on a piece of cardboard may cost as much as $350

The demand among collectors for the rookie cards of any athlete projected to reach superstar status typically runs high. (Got that, Moms?) But with Shaquille cards, there was a virtual feeding frenzy, a scene so full of intrigue that card shops were noting that as much as 90% of their business was in basketball cards. "That's all anybody is wanting," said one dealer. "And it's all because of Shaq."

Card companies customarily produce anywhere from one to three cards of a celebrated player. In Shaquille's case, some companies have produced as many as six or more. Generally available in foil, or wax packs, Shaquille's 'rookie cards' are selling for from $7 to $35 in card shops. A few harder-to-find, limited-print or random-insert cards may cost as much as $350.

Arrests were made when boxes containing a McDonald's premium Shaq card, made especially for the Central Florida area, turned up suspiciously at one card shop. The active, sometimes illicit trade in Shaq cards was made even more intriguing by the nearly 40 cards that were calling themselves Shaq's 'rookie card,' some of them produced by unlicensed maverick printers operating out of their garages. The wild rush sent the value of a few Shaq cards sky high. And all this, without anyone declaring which card was Shaq's official rookie card.

Perhaps only one person can put an end to the mystery.

FRIDAY, NOVEMBER 6
ORLANDO 110, MIAMI 100 (1-0)

Celebrated rookie Shaquille O'Neal made Orlando Arena the place to be opening night, but Nick Anderson and Dennis Scott made the night special for the Magic. Anderson scored a career-high 42 points; Scott added 27. O'Neal, with all the national hype surrounding him, quickly showed what all the fuss was about. He had 12 points, 18 rebounds and 3 blocked shots, providing a dominating force in the middle. He twice grabbed a defensive rebound and drove the length of the floor, once dunking and the other time dishing off for an assist.

SATURDAY, NOVEMBER 7
ORLANDO 103, WASHINGTON 93 (2-0)

Backup point guard Chris Corchiani scored 8 points in the final 5 minutes to spark the Magic. O'Neal provided inside muscle and led everyone with 22 points, 15 rebounds and 4 blocked shots at the Capital Centre in Landover, Maryland. Although he did most of his damage in the first half (16 points and 9 rebounds), O'Neal blocked a layup by Rex Chapman with 42 seconds left that could have closed the gap to one.

TUESDAY, NOVEMBER 10
CHARLOTTE 112, ORLANDO 108 (2-1)

O'Neal displayed his offensive potential, but there was a downside to his performance. Despite racking up 35 points (15 of 25 field goals), he was scoreless in the fourth quarter. He played 8 minutes and missed all 3 field goal attempts. The biggest miss came with 17 seconds left and the Magic trailing, 109-108. O'Neal dominated early, scoring 13 points in the first quarter and 15 in the third. "I don't know what happened in the fourth. Maybe I didn't get the ball enough. Maybe I wasn't working hard enough to get the ball," O'Neal said. "But I'll make no excuses. They stuck close the whole game, then capitalized on our mistakes."

THURSDAY, NOVEMBER 12
ORLANDO 127, WASHINGTON 100 (3-1)

The Magic, the second-worst team in the NBA a year ago, used the Washington Bullets as practice fodder. O'Neal, often double- and triple-teamed, again was impressive with 31 points, 21 rebounds and 4 blocked shots. "He just changes everything with his presence," Magic forward Jeff Turner said. "It makes it easier for everyone. With him in the game, the other team just doesn't want to get to the basket. They are happy to take jump shots, which can really get us going." Said O'Neal: "We had the killer instinct tonight. That was the difference. We came in tonight and wanted this one. We're not going to win them all, but we had the right attitude tonight."

SATURDAY, NOVEMBER 14
NEW JERSEY 124, ORLANDO 113 (3-2)

Force O'Neal out of the lineup and the Magic become an ordinary team. After luring the rookie into foul trouble, the New Jersey Nets coasted to victory at Brendan Byrne Arena. O'Neal picked up three fouls early and played 12 first-half minutes. O'Neal, who played all of the second half, made the score respectable en route to 29 points and 15 rebounds. He admitted the early fouls had a psychological impact. Said O'Neal: "Most of our games have been peaks and valleys, and then we come on in the end. Tonight, that didn't happen."

WEDNESDAY, NOVEMBER 18
ORLANDO 120, PHILADELPHIA 110 (4-2)

The Atlantic Division was beginning to look like a nice place to call home. For O'Neal, it certainly was a great place to start his career. The awesome rookie continued his early feast on Atlantic opponents, and the Magic strengthened their divisional lead by holding off the 76ers at The Spectrum. O'Neal had 29 points, 19 rebounds and 4 blocked shots. The rookie center and the league's leading rebounder got the right help at the right times. The only things that slowed him were foul trouble, which sent him to the bench, and his stamina, which still didn't appear to be NBA-caliber. O'Neal had 15 points and 10 rebounds by halftime. He tried to stay out of foul trouble in the second half. At the end of a big third quarter (13 points, 6 rebounds), he was assessed his fourth foul. He picked up his fifth with 4:16 remaining and the Magic up by six.

THURSDAY, NOVEMBER 19
ORLANDO 126, GOLDEN STATE 102 (5-2)

Against a team that won 55 games last season by using unusual lineups to create uncomfortable matchups, the Magic discovered something – they can do that too. Going small – provided O'Neal can stay in the game – can produce big results. With their ranks thin at power forward, the Magic used O'Neal and various combinations of small forwards and guards. O'Neal continued his assault on the league by getting 29 points, 16 rebounds and 3 blocked shots.

SATURDAY, NOVEMBER 21
NEW YORK 92, ORLANDO 77 (5-3)

O'Neal might have held a statistical edge in his celebrated first meeting at Madison Square Garden with six-time All-Star center Patrick Ewing, but it wasn't enough to overcome an otherwise lackluster team performance. Orlando, which came into the game averaging a league-leading 115.3 points per game, remained atop the Atlantic Division, but the team played mostly as if it belonged at the other end

Shaquille gets a 'spinal adjustment' in pre-game warmups from Dave Oliver, Magic strength and conditioning coach.

of the standings. The Knicks outrebounded, outfought and outlasted the Magic, who never really challenged for the lead except in a late surge that was quickly squelched. O'Neal had 18 points, 17 rebounds and 3 blocked shots – two against Ewing – even though he was pressing offensively and rushing his shots early in the game. Ewing had 15 points, 9 rebounds and 3 blocked shots, including one early against O'Neal. "I wanted it to be just me and Patrick going at it, but that's not the way the game is played," O'Neal said. "Each of us has four other guys around him. It's the Magic versus the Knicks, so he won this time. He's a great player. I'm a pretty good one."

WEDNESDAY, NOVEMBER 25
ORLANDO 107, HOUSTON 94 (6-3)

O'Neal doesn't have to score big for the Magic to win. He only has to play big, which he is learning even on his off-nights. The Magic proved that point at home – getting 30 points from Scott Skiles and 28 points from Dennis Scott. O'Neal, in a much-anticipated matchup with All-Star center Hakeem Olajuwon, started slowly and barely got into the offensive flow. Yet he remained a defensive force – changing shots and discouraging drives. His mere presence provided teammates with wide-open shots. O'Neal had 12 points, 13 rebounds and 3 blocked shots. Olajuwon had 22 points, 13 rebounds and 5 blocked shots. "I feel pretty good. Even when I'm not having a good scoring night, when my shots aren't falling, I can help us win," O'Neal said. "I know how to do some other things."

FRIDAY, NOVEMBER 27
ORLANDO 130, INDIANA 116 (7-3)

From the first day of training camp it was obvious that O'Neal would become something special. At this point, it was starting to look as if the Magic were pretty special too. All five starters scored 20 or more points. Point guard Scott Skiles, for the second game in a row, played all 48 minutes. The majority of the 48 were a treat for Orlando as he burned his former team at Market Square Arena for 32 points. O'Neal had 21 points and 11 rebounds.

SATURDAY, NOVEMBER 28
ORLANDO 95, CLEVELAND 93 (8-3)

Guard Nick Anderson hit a driving, twisting layup with 2.6 seconds to play, giving the Magic a victory that allowed the team to match their best month in history and keeping them atop the Atlantic Division. Anderson was an unlikely hero after struggling offensively. "I don't care about percentages. I could have missed all my shots before that point, and I still would have had the confidence. I was taking that ball in," he said. "I made the basket that counted." The Magic were led by Dennis Scott, who had 28 points and 9 rebounds. O'Neal had 22 points and 14 rebounds.

TUESDAY, DECEMBER 1
SEATTLE 116, ORLANDO 102 (8-4)

The Magic should have known they had traveled into trouble at The Coliseum when O'Neal had his first dunk attempt rudely rejected by Shawn Kemp, Seattle's own version of a young Superman. The SuperSonics, using a blue-collar approach to collaring O'Neal, had a superb second half to blast the Magic back to reality, 116-102, on the opening night of a three-game West Coast trip. O'Neal was held to 9 points and 11 rebounds, his least productive night to this point as an NBA player. The Sonics did it defensively with veteran center Michael Cage and Kemp, who combined to frustrate O'Neal. "I know it's just a matter of time before Shaq has his day against us, but I was fired up tonight," Cage said. "We wanted this one badly. We knew all about him coming in. That's all we've heard."

THURSDAY, DECEMBER 3
L.A. CLIPPERS 122, ORLANDO 104 (8-5)

The Clippers were playing in the shadow of the more glamorous, crosstown Lakers. But it sure looked a lot like Showtime against the Magic. It wasn't that the Clippers played wonderfully; it was the Magic who made them look so good at the Los Angeles Sports Arena. Orlando was led by O'Neal, who had 26 points and 9 rebounds. He won the statistical matchup with former college teammate and Clippers center Stanley

Roberts, but it was Roberts who surprised the Magic with some inspired play. He had a season-high 16 points, 6 rebounds and 3 blocked shots, including two early against O'Neal.

SATURDAY, DECEMBER 5
GOLDEN STATE 119, ORLANDO 104 (8-6)

The Magic dropped their third consecutive game, again playing without confidence and execution. The loss, coupled with victories by the New Jersey Nets and New York Knicks, dropped the Magic from first place to third in the Atlantic Division. O'Neal, who came into Oakland Coliseum Arena shooting 53 percent from the field, hit only 5 of 18 shots. He was in quick foul trouble, getting his fifth with 2:07 left in the third quarter. He hit 7 of 12 free throws finishing with 17 points and a game-high 17 rebounds and 6 blocks.

TUESDAY, DECEMBER 8
BOSTON 119, ORLANDO 104 (8-7)

Maybe they don't have Larry Bird anymore, but if the Celtics played like this every night, they won't miss him very much. The Celtics drilled the Magic, looking more like something from Boston's storied past than like a team struggling through a painful rebuilding process. The Magic hardly looked like the team that was riding high atop the Atlantic Division only 10 days ago. For the fourth consecutive game, they were hardly a factor in the fourth quarter. O'Neal had 26 points and 15 rebounds for the Magic, but the Celtics neutralized him enough with a variety of double teams from all angles.

WEDNESDAY, DECEMBER 9
DETROIT 108, ORLANDO 103 (8-8)

The Magic's shots were falling, but their defense went AWOL. The Pistons, behind guard Joe Dumars' 39 points, outlasted the Magic at The Palace. Orlando sank a team-record 14 3-pointers, with Dennis Scott, who had 38 points, making a club-record 8. The fireworks weren't enough though. The Magic gave up at least one basket for every one they scored, and O'Neal fouled out with 1:13 left. "There was a lot of hacking, a lot of actors [like Bill Laimbeer] out there too," O'Neal said. The Pistons successfully defended O'Neal, limiting him to 17 points and 11 rebounds. In the second half, he had just 3 points and 4 rebounds. Said O'Neal: "I don't think they were doing anything special. It was just a lot of hacking. There were a lot of rookie

calls out there. But I'll be a veteran one day."

FRIDAY, DECEMBER 11
PHOENIX 108, ORLANDO 107 (8-9)

O'Neal may well have been on the fast track to superstardom, but his free throws were spoiling all the fun. O'Neal missed 1 of 2 free throws with 6.5 seconds remaining, then did so again with 1.1 seconds left, allowing the Suns to escape with a victory. "I have no excuses. I just missed them," O'Neal said. "That sometimes happens to the best of them. I'll just have to hit the next one. At practice this morning I hit 20 in a row." Although O'Neal was fouled intentionally both times he touched the ball, neither play had been intended for him. Both times he was close enough to dunk, but had no chance with Suns hanging on his arms. O'Neal, who came into the game making 53.7 percent of his shots from the free-throw line, missed the first and hit the second to pull Orlando to 107-106 with 6.5 seconds to go. After Dan Majerle hit 1 of 2 for Phoenix less than a second later, O'Neal got another chance. He again made the first and missed the second free throw. Phoenix rebounded, and the game ended. O'Neal led the Magic with 26 points and 17 rebounds, including 6 on offense. He hit 10-of-18 shots and 6-of-10 from the line.

TUESDAY, DECEMBER 15
ORLANDO 119, PHILADELPHIA 107 (9-9)

The Magic used the 76ers' lack of inside strength to breeze to their first December victory since 1990. O'Neal scored 20 and grabbed 14 rebounds. The Sixers had no one to cope with O'Neal, who had 6 blocked shots and helped cause opposing center Andrew Lang to miss 7 of 8 field-goal attempts.

THURSDAY, DECEMBER 17
ORLANDO 112, SACRAMENTO 91 (10-9)

The Magic may not be as good as the top teams in the NBA, but they appeared a lot better than the clubs at the bottom. Orlando, leading from start to finish, rallied behind the play of O'Neal to trounce the Kings. O'Neal fell

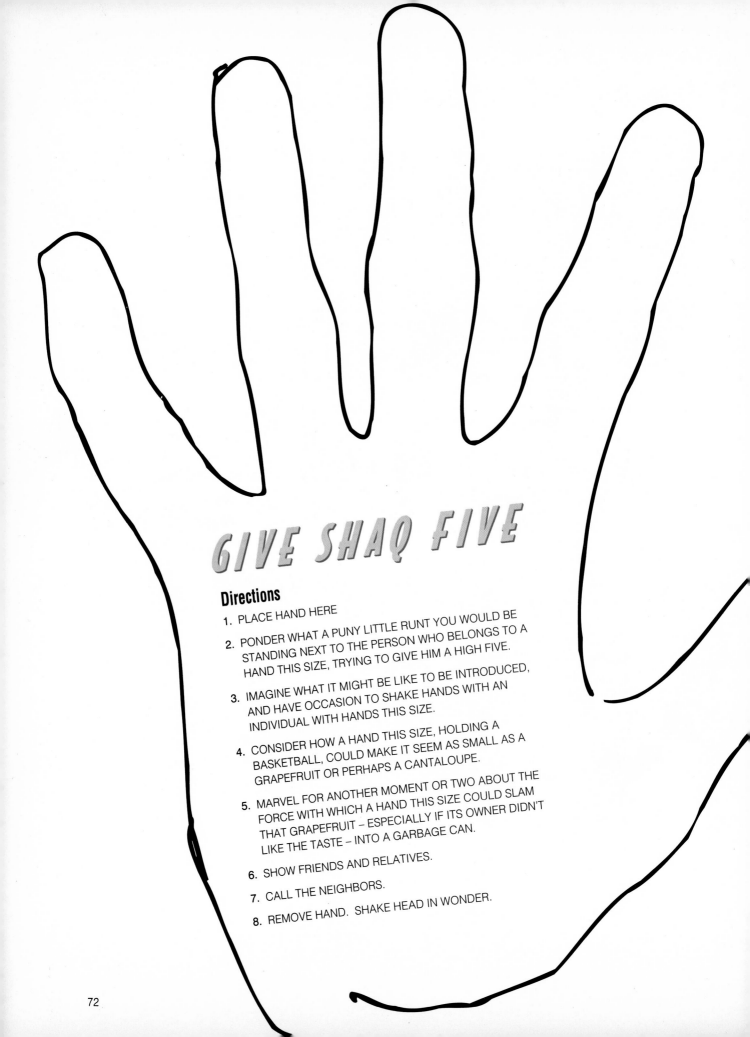

GIVE SHAQ FIVE

Directions

1. PLACE HAND HERE

2. PONDER WHAT A PUNY LITTLE RUNT YOU WOULD BE STANDING NEXT TO THE PERSON WHO BELONGS TO A HAND THIS SIZE, TRYING TO GIVE HIM A HIGH FIVE.

3. IMAGINE WHAT IT MIGHT BE LIKE TO BE INTRODUCED, AND HAVE OCCASION TO SHAKE HANDS WITH AN INDIVIDUAL WITH HANDS THIS SIZE.

4. CONSIDER HOW A HAND THIS SIZE, HOLDING A BASKETBALL, COULD MAKE IT SEEM AS SMALL AS A GRAPEFRUIT OR PERHAPS A CANTALOUPE.

5. MARVEL FOR ANOTHER MOMENT OR TWO ABOUT THE FORCE WITH WHICH A HAND THIS SIZE COULD SLAM THAT GRAPEFRUIT – ESPECIALLY IF ITS OWNER DIDN'T LIKE THE TASTE – INTO A GARBAGE CAN.

6. SHOW FRIENDS AND RELATIVES.

7. CALL THE NEIGHBORS.

8. REMOVE HAND. SHAKE HEAD IN WONDER.

3 blocked shots shy of what would have been his first NBA triple-double. Using his height and weight advantage to score easily against the Kings' smaller players, he had 22 points, 20 rebounds and 7 blocks. He grabbed 3 more rebounds than Sacramento's starting five combined, and the double- and triple-teams left Anderson and others open. Said O'Neal: "I just came out and played with a lot of intensity. We won against Philadelphia, and we wanted to keep the streak going."

SATURDAY, DECEMBER 19
ORLANDO 125, ATLANTA 84 (11-9)

With their leading scorer, Dominique Wilkins, on the bench in street clothes, his injured hand wrapped in a bandage, the rest of the Hawks played as if they were ailing too. Orlando, led by Dennis Scott's 28 points, put on a dazzling performance to trounce the Hawks at The Omni. It was the widest margin of victory in Orlando's brief history, and it was the most lopsided loss for the Hawks since a 44-point defeat to the Lakers in 1971. The Magic were so superior that O'Neal didn't have to do much – 15 points, 5 rebounds and 5 blocks. "They were a little flat, but I think early in the game they were concentrating on Shaquille so much," Scott said, "it just opened everything else up. In the second half, they got a little winded." O'Neal said he didn't try to force shots against the Hawks' double teams. "Common sense would tell you to try to find the open man," he said. "The shots were falling [for other players] tonight. Maybe if the shots weren't falling, I would have looked for my own shot a little more." The victory was the 200th of Orlando coach Matt Guokas' NBA career.

TUESDAY, DECEMBER 22
ORLANDO 101, UTAH 98 (12-9)

The bench that looked so bare a few games ago fed off the strength of O'Neal and carried the Magic past the Jazz. O'Neal and four reserves played almost the entire final period as the Magic won their fourth consecutive game, matching the longest winning streak in franchise history. With Litterial Green and Steve Kerr at guard, Donald Royal and Jeff Turner at forward and O'Neal at anchor, the Magic turned a 5-point deficit into a 9-point advantage, then fended off a late rally. "I wasn't going to yank them, because they were the ones who put us in position to win," Coach Guokas said. "They got the crowd into the game, and I think that rattled them [the Jazz]. We just got some giant contributions from a lot of people." O'Neal had 28 points, 19 rebounds and 5 blocked shots, including 3 in the fourth quarter when he seemed to raise his defense to a higher level. .

SATURDAY, DECEMBER 26
MIAMI 106, ORLANDO 100 (12-10)

The Magic started quickly and finished with a flurry, but they did little right in between in losing to the struggling Heat at Miami Arena. The Magic didn't rebound; they didn't play defense; they certainly didn't protect the ball. Yet they were close enough to challenge at the end. The ingredients that had gone into Orlando's four-game winning streak disappeared. Agressiveness was absent without explanation. Miami, which is not a good rebounding team, held a commanding 52-37 advantage, including 20 offensive rebounds. "We didn't rebound, and we didn't play defense," O'Neal said. "If you don't do those two things, you're not going to win very much." O'Neal had 18 points and 11 rebounds, but he hit only 6 of 15 shots.

MONDAY, DECEMBER 28
ORLANDO 110, MILWAUKEE 94 (13-10)

The Magic, good enough to capitalize on an uninspired opponent, pounded the Bucks. A lesson they learned in their troublesome loss at Miami – they can't win if they don't rebound – proved useful as the Magic took control late in the second quarter and never were challenged. O'Neal had 21 points and a game-high 14 rebounds.

WEDNESDAY, DECEMBER 30
L.A. LAKERS 96, ORLANDO 93 (13-11)

Opportunities at the end were there – actually everywhere – but the Magic failed to capitalize. O'Neal's franchise-record 23 rebounds were lost in an especially disappointing defeat as the Magic kicked away a game good teams normally win. "When we were up by eight, we should have put the nail in the coffin right there," O'Neal said. "There was no excuse. We just lost this one when we should have won." The big rookie had 23 points, but he also had seven turnovers. He failed to block a shot for the first time in his NBA career. With the Lakers up, 93-91, O'Neal traveled with 11 seconds left, dashing a chance to tie. "I thought that last traveling call was just a rookie call," O'Neal said. "Next year, I'll get that call. I'll be going to the free-throw line instead. But that's one of those things."

SATURDAY, JANUARY 2
DETROIT 98, ORLANDO 97 (13-12)

The Pistons remained unbeaten in four seasons against the Magic, as Joe Dumars scored 32 points, including 17 in a turnaround third quarter. O'Neal led the Magic with 29 points and 15 rebounds, but he was shut down by Dennis Rodman in the fourth quarter. O'Neal, Dennis Scott and Nick Anderson – each averaging more than 20 points per game – combined for just one point in the fourth quarter. That was an O'Neal free throw. He took only one shot. The Magic led, 50-38, at halftime with O'Neal and Anderson combining for 25 points. They led by as many as 15 points in the first quarter, turning a 6-6 tie into a 21-8 lead.

TUESDAY, JANUARY 5
NEW JERSEY 102, ORLANDO 99 (13-13)

This seven-game homestand – longest in franchise history – was expected to be a time when the Magic could assert themselves against some pretty good teams. Three games into it, the Magic fell flat. They failed to find any consistency down the stretch, where they could not make any big plays. Four times in the final 2:08 the Magic had the ball with the chance to at least tie, but each time they lost possession. The Nets won with an outside-inside attack of Drazen Petrovic and Derrick Coleman, who scored 29 and 28 points, respectively. O'Neal had 29 points and 12 rebounds for Orlando, getting 7 points in the final quarter before fouling out with 22 seconds remaining.

FRIDAY, JANUARY 8
ORLANDO 95, NEW YORK 94 (14-13)

The Knicks may be considered the most physical, most aggressive and best defensive team in the NBA, but O'Neal turned them into a group of pacifists with a dominating fourth-quarter performance. The Magic snapped a three-game losing streak and got a glimpse of the future with O'Neal's particularly inspired play. "He tried to block every shot, grab every rebound and score every point," Coach Guokas said. "He really did the job tonight. It was a strong fourth quarter." O'Neal had 11 points, 5 rebounds and 3 blocked shots in the final quarter, bringing the Magic back from a deficit – 79-67 – that had piled up in the third quarter while he was on the bench in foul trouble. He saved his best for last when the Knicks got a final chance at victory with 7 seconds remaining. O'Neal outfought Patrick Ewing for position near the basket, then with 2 seconds remaining, forced Ewing to take an off-balance jump hook that didn't come close . O'Neal grabbed the rebound, and time expired. Ewing said he had been fouled. "On the final play, he [O'Neal] got my body. He got my arm," Ewing said. "You name it, he got it. If it were the other way around, I'm sure they would have called the foul on me." O'Neal finished with 22 points,13 rebounds and 5 blocked shots. Ewing had 21 points, 12 rebounds and 1 blocked shot, hitting just 9 of 27 shots.

SATURDAY, JANUARY 9
INDIANA 104, ORLANDO 88 (14-14)

The Magic were pounded by the Pacers in a game in which they never challenged. The dreadful overall performance – probably the worst first half of the season – overshadowed another outstanding effort by O'Neal, who had 30 points, 20 rebounds and a franchise-record 8 blocked shots. O'Neal scored 15 consecutive points for the Magic in the second period. He blocked 3 consecutive shots on one possession by Indiana and a fourth on the next possession. His four blocked shots in the

second period tied a franchise record for blocks in a quarter. "It doesn't matter what I do individually," O'Neal said. "When we play like this, I feel like I let the team down,"

TUESDAY, JANUARY 12
CHICAGO 122, ORLANDO 106 (14-15)

Michael Jordan swept across the lane on the opening possession and swatted away the first shot by O'Neal. Just a superstar's welcome to the league. The Bulls, who had slipped into an early-season slump, returned to championship form. "He [Jordan] is the best," O'Neal said. "And they're a great team. They play well. They play hard. And they play together." O'Neal had 19 points, hitting 8 of 10 shots, 11 rebounds and a season-high 5 assists.

FRIDAY, JANUARY 15
ORLANDO 113, BOSTON 94 (15-15)

All those things that had gone so wrong during the Magic's recent homestand – defense, turnovers, shooting – suddenly went right at Boston Garden when the Magic won their first game in four seasons over the Celtics. The Magic snapped the Celtics' seven-game winning streak and played their best game in almost a month. The Celtics looked beaten emotionally long before the game was complete. O'Neal sent center Robert Parish into the second row of seats after blocking a shot in the third quarter. Parish climbed off the fans with ketchup on his shorts. O'Neal had 22 points, 12 rebounds and 4 blocked shots.

SATURDAY, JANUARY 16
ORLANDO 128, CHICAGO 124 (16-15)

The Magic saw Michael Jordan at his best, but they still beat the defending NBA champions in an overtime thriller at Chicago Stadium. Jordan scored 64 points, yet the Bulls dropped their second consecutive game to the Magic at Chicago in two seasons. Jordan, who had 53 points in one game against the Magic during the 1989 season, hit 26 of 47 shots – 5 points shy of his career high. It was the third time Jordan has scored at least 45 points against the Magic; each time the Bulls

have lost. Scott Skiles and O'Neal played exceptionally well. Skiles had 31 points and 10 assists. O'Neal had 29 points and a team-record 24 rebounds.

MONDAY, JANUARY 18
PHILADELPHIA 124, ORLANDO 118 (16-16)

The Magic allowed a monster game by O'Neal to mean very little, losing in overtime to the 76ers at The Spectrum. O'Neal had a career-high 38 points, 16 rebounds and 8 blocked shots. He altered at least 10 other shots. The Magic trailed by 11 when the fourth quarter began, but that's when Philadelphia's shooting suddenly went cold and O'Neal accelerated. He had 9 points, 6 rebounds and 3 blocks as the Magic fought back. "We gave ourselves a chance to win, but we just couldn't pull it out," O'Neal said. "I should have scored 50 today. When you lose, it doesn't really matter what you did."

FRIDAY, JANUARY 22
MIAMI 110, ORLANDO 104 (16-17)

The Heat should have pitched a tent at the free-throw line. It certainly seemed as if they made their living there. Miami set records for a Magic opponent by taking 52 free throws and by making 44, including six in a row in the final 1:03 that sealed Orlando's fate. The Heat, who had the worst record in the Eastern Conference, used big games from Glen Rice and Steve Smith to snap a four-game losing streak. The victory boosted their series record to 9-4. Personal fouls against O'Neal proved costly. He had 15 points and 11 rebounds, but he played a season-low 24 minutes.

SATURDAY, JANUARY 23
ORLANDO 127, DALLAS 106 (17-17)

Playing the Mavericks – winless on the road – was a lot like picking cherries. There wasn't much resistance. The Magic plucked the Mavericks as O'Neal tied his career high with 38 points, hitting 14 of 16 shots. He also had 13 rebounds and seven blocks in 40 minutes and left the game at 4:10 without a foul for the first time in the season. "We put the nail in the coffin early," O'Neal said. "As a player, you look at their record and you know they have some problems. But considering that, we still came out and played hard. I tried to treat this like another game."

TUESDAY, JANUARY 26
ORLANDO 120, ATLANTA 106 (18-17)

Six-time NBA All-Star Dominique Wilkins had a game-high 27 points, but he was ambushed from so many angles his head was spinning as the Orlando Magic breezed to victory over the Hawks. Orlando starters had their day: O'Neal had 26 points and 12 rebounds; Skiles had 22 points and 11 assists; Nick Anderson had 20 points, 6 rebounds and 7 assists; Anthony Bowie had 20 points, 7 rebounds and 7 assists, the latter two season highs. It was the second time this season all starters scored at least 20 points.

THURSDAY, JANUARY 28
CLEVELAND 127, ORLANDO 113 (18-18)

It's not only playing well that counts in the NBA; it's also knowing when to play well. The Cavaliers knew when to play well. They unraveled Orlando in the final minutes at The Coliseum and sped away with a comfortable victory. The ball stopped going inside to O'Neal, the Magic stopped playing defense, and they became sloppy and impatient on offense. O'Neal, who was in foul trouble again, had 25 points but only 7 rebounds, 7 below his average. He played 34 minutes and had just 5 points in the fourth quarter.

FRIDAY, JANUARY 29
BOSTON 116, ORLANDO 105 (18-19)

It was a fight for the Celtics to force overtime but a breeze to win it. They capitalized on the premature departure of O'Neal as an invitation to do as they pleased. O'Neal fouled out 27 seconds into overtime with the score tied. Without O'Neal blocking their path, the Celtics outscored the Magic, 17-6, going 7 of 8 from the field. Most of the points came from inside. The Magic offered little resistance without their prize rookie. "Things just seem to change a little when I'm not out there,"

O'Neal said. "Guys penetrate more. I need to keep myself in the game." He had 26 points, 13 rebounds and 2 blocked shots.

MONDAY, FEBRUARY 1
ORLANDO 119, SACRAMENTO 115 (19-19)

With O'Neal on the sideline in foul trouble much of the fourth quarter, the Magic turned a 14-point deficit into a surprising victory at ARCO Arena. Using a small lineup that seemed sparked by O'Neal's absence, the Magic opened a five-game West Coast trip with a much-needed boost of confidence. O'Neal picked up his fifth personal foul – and went to the bench – with 9:12 remaining and the Magic down by 11. When Lionel Simmons immediately completed a 3-point play, things looked dim for the Magic. "We just kept our poise this time," Magic guard Nick Anderson said. "When the big guy went out, everyone just picked it up." Anderson led the Magic with 31 points and 14 rebounds. O'Neal returned at 3:39 with the Magic down by one. He fouled out 20 seconds later. O'Neal, often frustrated by the double- and triple-teams, finished with 18 points and a season-low 6 rebounds.

TUESDAY, FEBRUARY 2
ORLANDO 110, L.A. LAKERS 97 (20-19)

The lights of Hollywood went on, and O'Neal turned it on, leading the Magic past the Lakers. It was the first victory for the Magic at The Forum. The Lakers, once so impressive, looked so uninspired. O'Neal had 31 points and 14 rebounds, dampening any enthusiasm the Lakers might have had around the basket. More than once, he made a big play and then delivered a wink or a smile to one of the movie types sitting courtside. "I'm glad I had a good game here," O'Neal said. "There is a lot of tradition in this building, and it means something to play well here."

FRIDAY, FEBRUARY 5
ORLANDO 114, PORTLAND 106 (21-19)

The longest road trip of the season turned into the most successful stretch of road in team history as the Magic leveled the Trail Blazers at Memorial Coliseum. It was the first time in their four

seasons the Magic won three consecutive road games. It was their ninth road victory of the season, the most in team history. It matched last season's victory total (21 games) and marked the first time in nine games the Magic have beaten the Blazers. O'Neal, who had 22 points and 11 rebounds, said, "We're on this road trip with an us-against-the-world attitude."

SUNDAY, FEBRUARY 7
PHOENIX 121, ORLANDO 105 (21-20)

The Magic might have lost the game but the unprecedented hype surrounding O'Neal rose another notch as he tore down a goal standard in the NBA's most modern arena. The Suns ended the Magic's modest road winning streak as they scored 44 points in the fourth quarter at America West Arena. O'Neal's first-quarter dunk and the subsequent basket collapse stopped the game for 37 minutes, but he couldn't stop the Suns from his seat on the bench as foul trouble dogged him once more. He played just 2 minutes of the final quarter. The timing of his Herculean feat couldn't have been better – it came during the first network television appearance in Magic history. "I thought a lot of calls against me today were questionable. But that's okay. I'm a rookie, and they [the officials] have never seen anyone like me. I'll get those calls next year." O'Neal played just 29 minutes, getting 20 points and a season-low 5 rebounds.

MONDAY, FEBRUARY 8
UTAH 108, ORLANDO 96 (21-21)

Orlando saved its worst for last: A road-weary performance at the Delta Center against the Jazz. O'Neal blocked two of Utah forward Karl Malone's shots but found himself in foul trouble again. "I thought we were kind of physically and mentally tired tonight," he said. "Way too many mistakes." O'Neal had 22 points and 11 rebounds.

WEDNESDAY, FEBRUARY 10
ORLANDO 96, CLEVELAND 87 (22-21)

The Cavaliers have led the league in All-Star selections (three), but the Magic gave them no respect. Orlando, showing no signs of fatigue, smothered the Cavs at one end of the floor and breezed at the other. The Magic surpassed last season's victory total of 21 and matched last season's home court total of 13. O'Neal had 19 points and 14 rebounds despite playing with the flu and needing medical attention after the game.

THURSDAY, FEBRUARY 11
CHARLOTTE 116, ORLANDO 107 (22-22)

Rookie centers Alonzo Mourning and O'Neal battled to nearly a statistical draw in what could become a classic matchup. They battled with the tenacity of prize fighters. But Mourning, playing with a heavily bandaged left thumb, enjoyed the edge that counted most: His team won. Charlotte, which broke for 45 fast-break points, took control early in the fourth quarter and held on at Charlotte Coliseum. The Hornets improved to 2-0 this season against the Magic. O'Neal, playing despite the flu, had 29 points, 15 rebounds and 4 blocked shots. Mourning, playing with a broken bone under his left thumbnail, had 27 points, 14 rebounds and 2 blocks. "It will be the battle of the future – O'Neal versus Mourning," O'Neal said. "It was a good battle this time. They walked away with the win. We just have to get them next time."

SUNDAY, FEBRUARY 14
ORLANDO 102, NEW YORK 100 (23-22)

In a game that resembled mud wrestling – or maybe a tractor pull – the Magic slogged to a triple-overtime victory on national TV against the Knicks. Foregoing finesse in favor of forced entry, the Magic matched the Knicks' down-and-dirty style every step of the way. O'Neal struggled offensively but rose up at the end to dominate like a superstar. Playing with a sore lower back and lingering effects of the flu, O'Neal blocked a shot by Patrick Ewing at the end of regulation and then blocked six more in overtime. The rookie made only 3 of 17 shots in regulation but 5 of 8 field-goal attempts in overtime for 13 points, including the only 4 points the Magic scored in the third extra period. "I had a horrible game offensively today," said O'Neal, who finished with

21 points, 19 rebounds and a team-record 9 blocks. "But I understand there are more ways to help this team. I wanted a victory, regardless of how it looked." At the end of regulation, O'Neal muscled Ewing away from the basket and then stuffed Ewing's shot that could have won the game just before the buzzer. Then he helped tie up Anthony Mason in the closing seconds of the first overtime, preventing a last-second shot. He blocked a shot by John Starks with seconds remaining at the end of the second overtime. He blocked three in the third, including one by Herb Williams with 36 seconds remaining, which could have tied the game.

TUESDAY, FEBRUARY 16
DETROIT 124, ORLANDO 120 (23-23)

A 46-point, 21-rebound performance by O'Neal was wasted at The Palace free-throw line. Towering over other players and twisting through double-teams for dunks and layups, O'Neal did everything right except sink his free throws – and the Magic lost in overtime. O'Neal missed 4 free throws in the final minute of regulation, including one that would have put the Magic ahead with 5.1 seconds left. His layup made it 113-113, and he was fouled on the play. But O'Neal missed the free throw, and time ran out in the scramble for the rebound. O'Neal's problems from the line continued in overtime. He missed 2 foul shots with 2:40 left and the Magic trailing, 119-115. For the game, he was 8 of 16 from the line, but he missed 7 of his last 9 starting with 1:04 left in regulation. He offered no excuses. "I just missed them," he said. He took the loss hard. "Maybe it was my fault. I think it is," he said. "The next time I get that opportunity, I'm going to hit those shots." At this point in the schedule, the Pistons remained the only team the Magic had not beaten. Detroit is 4-0 against the Magic, including 3-0 this season.

WEDNESDAY, FEBRUARY 17
ORLANDO 111, DENVER 99 (24-23)

The Magic blasted the Nuggets, deciding the outcome with a 16-0 run at the start of the second half. After building a 21-point lead midway in the third quarter, they never were challenged.

Orlando used a balanced attack – with five players scoring between 17 and 24 points – and good second-half shooting to move back above .500 at the All-Star break. "It was a good way to end the first half," Magic coach Matt Guokas said. "We're probably right where we should be, for the way we've been playing." O'Neal had 24 points and 18 rebounds.

TUESDAY, FEBRUARY 23
ORLANDO 125, PORTLAND 107 (25-23)

Recharged by the All-Star break and revolving around their All-Star center, the Magic completed a season sweep of the Trail Blazers. O'Neal looked like the All-Star he was with 28 points, 14 rebounds and 5 blocked shots. The Magic set a franchise record by hitting 62.2 percent (45 of 74) from the field. The Magic outscored the Blazers, 46-22, in the third period, which effectively settled the outcome.

THURSDAY, FEBRUARY 25
CHICAGO 108, ORLANDO 106 (25-24)

Unlike the last time they played, there was no miraculous finish to this late rally. Michael Jordan killed that storyline. The Bulls, after leading almost the entire game, fought off a late surge by the Magic and hung onto Jordan's cape for the victory. Jordan – despite a bad ankle – scored a game-high 36 points, including 6 of Chicago's last 8 points. "If the Magic could have pulled out this one, who knows what it would have done for their confidence," Bulls center Will Perdue said. While O'Neal had 30 points and 19 rebounds – keeping the game respectable throughout – it was Scott Skiles who led a furious comeback. Skiles was virtually perfect in the fourth when he had 13 points, hitting all three of his 3-point attempts, and all four of his free throws. "I think that says a lot about us," O'Neal said. "We were down by 20 [24], but no one was pointing any fingers. We didn't quit. We can play with anyone when we keep with it."

FRIDAY, FEBRUARY 26
ORLANDO 92, WASHINGTON 91 (26-24)

Nick Anderson, stripped of the

basketball just seconds earlier, sank a 3-point shot off the Capital Centre back board with 1.8 seconds left. The Magic appeared headed for an embarrassing loss after LaBradford Smith stole the ball from Anderson with 12 seconds left. Orlando was forced to foul after Anderson's turnover, and Bullets guard Michael Adams went to the free-throw line with 4.4 seconds left. Adams made 1 of 2 free throws to give Washington a 91-89 lead. The Magic called a timeout to get the ball at halfcourt. Using O'Neal as a decoy, Orlando drew the Bullets' defense in close and fed the ball to Anderson near the top of the key. He immediately shot from 27 feet, and the ball banged low off the backboard and through the rim. "Orlando's shot was lucky,'" Bullets coach Wes Unseld said. Replied Anderson: "Luck only counts in horseshoes." O'Neal had a game-high 28 points and 11 rebounds.

SUNDAY, FEBRUARY 28
SAN ANTONIO 94, ORLANDO 90 (26-25)

Nick Anderson called it a lack of pregame concentration. Anthony Bowie said everyone seemed distracted. O'Neal said he might have been too eager to do well. Whatever the reason, the result was a loss. The Magic fell behind quickly and decisively, then spent much of the game futilely playing catch-up. The Magic got poor shooting from just about everyone, including

Anderson, who still scored a game-high 30 points. "We need to quit screwing around during pregame," Anderson said. O'Neal finished with 19 points, 13 rebounds and 3 blocked shots. He spent much of the game in foul trouble.

TUESDAY, MARCH 2
ORLANDO 108, MINNESOTA 89 (27-25)

A second-half scoring frenzy by reserve forward Jeff Turner – 16 points in a span of 5 minutes, 32 seconds – sparked Orlando. Although the Magic never trailed after the first quarter, Turn-er pulled them out of a third-quarter funk and allowed them to coast home on a high with a tough part of the schedule – eight of the next 11 games on the road – about to begin. O'Neal had 25 points, 16 rebounds and 2 blocked shots, but it was Turner who turned the tide when the Timberwolves threatened to make it a game again. Minnesota had cut Orlando's 14-point lead to 5 as the third period ended. But behind Turner, the Magic quickly went up by 17. "I may be the man here," O'Neal said. "But Jeff Turner was the man tonight."

THURSDAY, MARCH 4
NEW JERSEY 116, ORLANDO 97 (27-26)

The Magic, who braved a fierce storm en route to the Meadowlands Arena, seemed to have nothing left for

the Nets. The Magic's best moves might have taken place in the parking lot as they withstood powerful winds after stepping off the team bus. Orlando was outrebounded, 47-25, and it would prove to be the team's most lopsided loss of the season. It was an all-time rebounding low for the Magic. O'Neal was unable to dominate because of foul trouble. He finished with 18 points, 11 rebounds and a game-high 8 blocked shots.

FRIDAY, MARCH 5
MILWAUKEE 109, ORLANDO 91 (27-27)

While the road trip began at the Bradley Center with high hopes, Orlan-do lost its second game in a row. The Bucks took control behind point guard Eric Murdock. The Magic also lost Den-nis Scott to an injury. He had to leave the game because of Achilles' tendini-tis. O'Neal was held in check again. He scored 18 points and had 10 rebounds.

SUNDAY, MARCH 7
ORLANDO 112, L.A. CLIPPERS 95 (28-27)

With the security of a new contract and the confidence that the ball was coming his way, Nick Anderson responded with 36 points and 8 rebounds, leading the Magic past the Clippers. In his first home game since signing his lucrative contract extension

– a day after the team's first players-only meeting of the season – Anderson carried the Magic through a quick start and an equally strong finish. He hit 14 of 21 shots (66.7 percent) and 2 of 3 from 3-point range. The Magic's performance spoiled the return of Clippers center Stanley Roberts, who was traded from Orlando during the summer. Roberts showed flashes of talent, but he couldn't sustain it. He had 12 points, 6 rebounds and 3 blocked shots. He fouled out with 33 seconds remaining. O'Neal had 23 points, 15 rebounds and 3 blocked shots.

MONDAY, MARCH 8
NEW YORK 109, ORLANDO 107 (28-28)

Orlando, with O'Neal fouling out in the fourth quarter, lost to New York in overtime. It was the last meeting of the season between the clubs. New York forced a 2-2 split of the series, with both teams winning twice on their courts. The Knicks held on behind center Patrick Ewing's 37 points, including 23 in the first half, 16 in the first quarter. Ewing also had 17 rebounds to win his personal battle against O'Neal. The rookie had 23 points and nine rebounds but was only 8 for 23 from the field. "I definitely wanted this one badly," Ewing said. "We were going up against a premier center. We've lost to them the last two times we've played them." This time, O'Neal fouled out with 15.4 seconds left in regulation.

WEDNESDAY, MARCH 10
ORLANDO 119, INDIANA 106 (29-28)

The Magic capitalized on a big fourth quarter – 10 points and 6 rebounds – from forward Tom Tolbert to stay ahead of the Pacers in the race for the seventh Eastern Conference playoff position. A front line of O'Neal and Tolbert was too much for the Pacers, especially down the stretch. Almost every time the Pacers double-teamed O'Neal, there was Tolbert, waiting to pick up the rebound, scramble for a loose ball or hit an open shot. O'Neal had 26 points and 11 rebounds. Tolbert, normally left to do the dirty work, had 22 points and 13 rebounds. "That's not the first time I outrebounded Shaq," Tolbert said with

a laugh. "And he'll still tell me it can't happen."

FRIDAY, MARCH 12
ATLANTA 110, ORLANDO 92 (29-29)

The Hawks, embarrassed earlier by the Magic, drilled them decisively this time. Veterans Dominique Wilkins and Kevin Willis had a do-as-you-please night, using the Magic like practice fodder on the Omni floor. Wilkins had 35 points and 9 assists. Willis had 26 points and 17 rebounds. The Magic were flat at the beginning and grew worse. Nick Anderson had 33 points and hit 13 of 23 shots. O'Neal, who hit just 7 of 20 shots, had 22 points and 13 rebounds.

SUNDAY, MARCH 14
SEATTLE 105, ORLANDO 97 (29-30)

The Magic, who have led the NBA in turnovers nearly all season, showed why against the SuperSonics in advance of a four-game western road swing. Orlando committed 18 turnovers and fumbled away control of the game in the final five minutes. The Magic had trouble passing to players who were wide open. Twice, passes sailed over the heads of players standing alone beyond the 3-point line. Even with those difficulties, the Magic still were in position to win, thanks in part to an 8-0 rally at the start and Nick Anderson's 17 points in the first period. But the Magic fell apart late in the game. Anderson cooled off, scoring 9 points over the final three quarters to finish with 26. O'Neal, who had 29 points and 8 rebounds, said the Magic had considered this a "must" game. "We just didn't take care of the ball, and it resulted in a loss," he said.

TUESDAY, MARCH 16
HOUSTON 94, ORLANDO 93 (29-31)

The Rockets, who trailed almost the entire game, rode offensive rebounding in the final quarter to a come-from-behind victory over the Magic at the Summit. It was a franchise-record 14th consecutive victory for the Rockets, who shot 44 percent from the field while missing six of their final eight field goals. But they also managed 5 offensive rebounds during

that stretch. In the fourth quarter, they outscored the Magic, 12-0, in points off turnovers and 9-0 in second-chance points. Despite their breakdowns, the Magic still had an opportunity to win when Nick Anderson stole a pass by Hakeem Olajuwon with 10 seconds remaining, setting up a 15-foot shot by Litterial Green that missed with 2 seconds left. O'Neal had 16 points and 17 rebounds, but he scored just two points in the fourth quarter. Hakeem Olajuwon had 20 points, 15 rebounds and 9 assists.

WEDNESDAY, MARCH 17
DALLAS 102, ORLANDO 96 (29-32)

The Magic couldn't stop the NBA's longest winning streak in Houston, but they stopped an even more remarkable streak. The lowly Mavericks snapped a 19-game losing skid – one away from tying the single-season NBA record – by beating the Magic at Reunion Arena. Orlando, leading by 4 at the start of the fourth quarter, collapsed after point guard Scott Skiles left the game with a slight shoulder separation and 11:40 remaining. Dallas (5-57) made a 17-3 run that led to the victory. The Mavs held a 43-37 rebounding advantage. Orlando's offense got so bad that O'Neal went 15:05 through the third and fourth quarters without a field-goal attempt. He had only three attempts in the second half in 20 minutes. "The Mavericks didn't stop me," O'Neal said. "I hardly shot. We took a lot of jump shots. What else can I say. It was nothing Dallas did." Nick Anderson led the Magic with 25 points, 8 rebounds and 5 steals. O'Neal had 21 points and 12 rebounds.

FRIDAY, MARCH 19
SAN ANTONIO 96, ORLANDO 93 (29-33)

It was a bittersweet return to his hometown for O'Neal, who was ejected midway in the fourth quarter of a loss to the Spurs. O'Neal, who had bought 500 tickets for family and friends, was ejected after back-to-back technical fouls. He disputed an offensive foul. "I can't comment on the officials, but I just think somebody wanted me out of the game," O'Neal said. "Whoever that was, I don't know." His ejection came in the midst

of a terrible stretch of play for the Magic. He left with 15 points and 13 rebounds and the Magic trailing, 81-69, with 6:45 remaining. The Magic fell further behind, 88-69, before staging a rally. The Spurs opened the fourth quarter with a 17-2 run – 23-2 counting the end of the third quarter. The Magic responded with a 24-6 spurt that closed the gap to 94-93 with 11 seconds remaining. The Spurs' Sean Elliott rounded out the scoring with two free throws. O'Neal had two offensive fouls within a minute in the fourth, the last leading to his ejection. Both calls came against center David Robinson, who led everyone with 30 points and 7 rebounds. Official Darell Garretson, head of the NBA's officiating staff, made the charging call against O'Neal, then called the first technical. After trotting downcourt, before play resumed, he was called for a second technical by official Tim Nunez, who was close to him at the other end. "Both of the technical fouls were for unsportsmanlike comments," Garretson said. O'Neal said he was talking to himself when he

received the second technical. "No way was that a charging call," he said. "I was just making a strong move to the basket. They are trying to break me, but I won't break."

SATURDAY, MARCH 20
ORLANDO 114, DENVER 108 (30-33)

The Magic were on the other end of things when they snapped a five-game losing streak by beating the Nuggets at McNichols Arena. The Magic avoided a four-game road sweep, which would have threatened their playoff hopes. Nick Anderson scored 32 points, including 8 in the last six minutes when the Magic staved off the Nuggets' final charge. Reserve Donald Royal also played big, getting 25 points by hitting 7 of 10 shots and 11 of 13 free throws. Although O'Neal was in foul trouble much of the game, he had 22 points, 9 rebounds and 2 blocked shots in 29 minutes. Denver center Dikembe Mutombo had the same problem; he finished with 15 points and 7 rebounds.

TUESDAY, MARCH 23
ORLANDO 103, MIAMI 89 (31-33)

It was just one victory and it didn't move them anywhere in the standings – but the Magic cleared a psychological hurdle by drubbing the Heat. Although they recently had looked like a team on the slide, the Magic seemed to regain the playoff mentality that had been slipping away. "Every game we play now has playoff implications," Coach Guokas said. "You can't get too high from a win or too low from a loss, but right now we're looking to get on a roll." Orlando used a 14-0 run to start the second half and maintained control. O'Neal came up big with 28 points and 10 rebounds.

FRIDAY, MARCH 26
CHICAGO 107, ORLANDO 86 (31-34)

The Bulls put away their fun-and-games, regular-season attitude and replaced it with their playoff face. The Magic never stood a chance. There were no gaudy numbers, no individual

standouts – just the efficiency that is expected from a quality team. The lead went from 10 points early in the third period to 20 in little time. The loss dropped the Magic two games behind Indiana for the eighth and final Eastern Conference playoff spot. O'Neal led the Magic with 20 points and 7 rebounds, but 12 of his points came in the first quarter. The Bulls, who won their sixth consecutive game, were led by Scottie Pippen with 20 points and 13 rebounds. Michael Jordan, who earlier had 64 points against the Magic in a losing cause, made 18 points.

SATURDAY, MARCH 27
ORLANDO 98, NEW JERSEY 84 (32-34)

Point guard Scott Skiles, once feared lost for the rest of the season, returned from a left shoulder separation. Adding him to Orlando's lineup was like placing a new engine in a car: Everything ran more smoothly. The Magic, with Skiles playing all 48 minutes, beat New Jersey for the first time in the season. Skiles had 21 points and 9 rebounds, but having Dennis Scott on the floor for 30 minutes was just as significant. Troubled by injuries, Scott appeared healthy despite shooting only 4 of 13 from the field. It was his third game back and his longest stretch of playing time since returning from

Achilles' tendinitis in his right leg. O'Neal had 27 points and 17 rebounds, clearly outplaying New Jersey's Derrick Coleman. Coleman, who had averaged 30.7 points in three previous contests this season against Orlando, had 16 points and 10 rebounds.

TUESDAY, MARCH 30
ORLANDO 105, DETROIT 91 (33-34)

The Magic survived a finish filled with fireworks – including the second ejection of O'Neal from a game – to finally beat the Pistons. O'Neal was tossed for punching Pistons guard Alvin Robertson with 2:13 remaining and the Magic ahead by 12 points. The victory was the first after 14 losses in four seasons over the Pistons. The Magic now had beaten every team in the league at least one time. O'Neal left the game with a season-low 7 points, frustrated because of the Pistons' strategy to intentionally foul him on every possession in the closing minutes. Isiah Thomas, who led everyone with 32 points, was ejected with 2:52 remaining after getting back-to-back technical fouls for disputing a foul call against Robertson. Robertson, on the Pistons' next possession after O'Neal's ejection, was ejected for throwing Scott Skiles to the floor as they jockeyed for position. Skiles, who played 48 minutes for the second consecutive game, led the Magic with 27 points and seven assists. Dennis Scott had 26 points in a reserve role. Nick Anderson had 24 points and 8 rebounds.

THURSDAY, APRIL 1
CHARLOTTE 102, ORLANDO 93 (33-35)

It was a franchise flashback. This was the way the Magic looked before the arrival of O'Neal. And the result was no surprise. Playing without O'Neal for the first time in the season – he was serving a one-game league-imposed suspension for fighting – the Magic lost at home to the Hornets. The loss dropped the Magic out of the final Eastern Conference playoff position, and it firmed up the Hornets' hold on the seventh spot. Charlotte center Alonzo Mourning led everyone with 30 points, 9 rebounds and 3 blocked shots. The

Magic were without Nick Anderson, their second-leading scorer, in the second half. He left the game at halftime with the flu. Without O'Neal, the Magic alternated Greg Kite and Brian Williams at center, and even used them together at times. Both played well, recording season highs in points and rebounds: Kite had 10 points and 10 rebounds, Williams had 14 points and 9 rebounds. Scott Skiles led the Magic with 23 points and 14 rebounds in 46 minutes. Dennis Scott had 20 points.

FRIDAY, APRIL 2
INDIANA 118, ORLANDO 102 (33-36)

O'Neal's return to the Magic lineup didn't change the problem that threatened to end the Orlando Magic's playoff hopes. The Pacers beat the Magic by dominating around the basket. "It's been a problem all season," Magic coach Matt Guokas said. "And when we break down inside, nothing seems to work. It takes all the starch out of us." Orlando was outrebounded, 53-40, despite O'Neal's game-high 19. The loss knocked the Magic 1 1/2 games behind in the race for the final playoff spot with 13 games remaining. It was O'Neal's first game after serving his suspension. He had 28 points. Nick Anderson led everyone with 32 points. For the first time all season he didn't start (flu).

SUNDAY, APRIL 4
MIAMI 124, ORLANDO 106 (33-37)

The Magic lost their third consecutive game, this time to the Heat. The loss left them tied with Detroit in ninth place but only 1 1/2 games away from Miami and 11th place in the Eastern Conference. Steve Smith led Miami with a career-high 31 points and 9 assists. The Magic, who had 19 turnovers, never led. A third-quarter rally did trim an 18-point deficit to 1. Nick Anderson had 27 points and 10 rebounds. O'Neal had 18 points and 10 rebounds, but he had just 1 point in the final 17 minutes. He took only one shot in the final quarter. He had 6 turnovers. It marked the first time in almost three months that the Magic had Anderson and Dennis Scott in the starting lineup at the same time. Scott had only 3 points in 23 minutes.

TUESDAY, APRIL 6
ORLANDO 116, PHILADELPHIA 90 (34-37)

If only it were this easy every night. The Magic emerged from a three-game losing streak to blast the 76ers in the first of six remaining games against teams already eliminated from playoff contention. The Magic, who remained a game behind Indiana for the last Eastern Conference playoff spot, took control midway through the second quarter and never were challenged. O'Neal led everyone with 35 points – 22 in the first half – and 16 rebounds. "We had a lot of fun out there tonight," Magic guard Nick Anderson said. "I don't think they wanted anything to do with Shaq." O'Neal virtually did as he pleased, hitting 17 of 23 shots from the field in 35

minutes. Unlike most of the Magic's opponents, the Sixers elected not to double-team him in the first half. "When they don't double-team me, that's just an invitation to dunk," O'Neal said. "When it's one-on-one, I just take it to him, whoever it is." O'Neal had 13 dunks but shot only 2 free throws.

WEDNESDAY, APRIL 7
ORLANDO 109, CHARLOTTE 96 (35-37)

O'Neal left no doubt about who should be the NBA's Rookie of the Year. His 29 points and 10 rebounds against Alonzo Mourning led the Magic. It was the first time in four games the Magic had beaten Charlotte this season. Mourning, who had 21 points and 8 rebounds, would go on to finish second in the rookie voting. O'Neal clearly had the edge in this matchup. He was a bigger threat on offense and more intim-

idating on defense. He had three blocked shots. Mourning had no blocks. Neither player would talk much about the matchup. "I would like to win the Rookie of the Year award," O'Neal said. "But if I don't get it, life goes on." Mourning, who made virtually no comments about O'Neal, said the Magic played better as a team. "They hit some big shots, and they outrebounded us too," he said.

FRIDAY, APRIL 9
ORLANDO 95, MINNESOTA 92 (36-37)

A clutch shot by Nick Anderson kept Orlando's playoff hopes alive. Anderson's 12-foot jumper with 2.2 seconds left lifted the Magic to a thrilling victory over the Timberwolves. Orlando pulled one game behind the Indiana Pacers, who were idle, in the Eastern Conference standings. Indiana was in eighth place – holding down the final playoff berth in the East. While Anderson was the hero, Minnesota's Chuck Person was the goat. Person added to the drama after Anderson's shot, which made the score 94-92. Person, aware that his team had exhausted its supply of timeouts, persisted in asking for another. The Timberwolves were granted a timeout – and a technical foul. Orlando's Scott Skiles sank the free throw to make it 95-92. The ball returned to the T-Wolves and a desperation shot by Doug West failed at the buzzer. O'Neal led Orlando with 29 points and 9 rebounds. Fellow rookie Christian Laettner had 20 for the Timberwolves.

SATURDAY, APRIL 10
MILWAUKEE 107, ORLANDO 98 (36-38)

With injured starters Nick Anderson and Tom Tolbert on the bench, the Magic wasted a great opportunity to advance in the standings. Because Indiana had lost to Chicago, the Magic could have gained on the Pacers in the Eastern Conference playoff race. But Orlando lost, enabling the Pacers, who held the eighth playoff spot, to cling to a one-game lead over the Magic. The Detroit Pistons moved a half-game ahead of Orlando into the No. 9 position. Orlando was No. 10. The Magic,

now 0-8 in games played at Milwaukee, sorely missed Anderson, who couldn't play because of a strained right hamstring, and Tolbert, who was out with a sprained left ankle. Milwaukee broke the game open in the fourth period. The score was 77-77 at the start of the quarter, but O'Neal was on the bench with five fouls. By the time he returned with 5:47 to play, the Magic had fallen behind, 92-83. They never came close to catching up. O'Neal finished with 20 points and 16 rebounds in 33 minutes.

TUESDAY, APRIL 13
ORLANDO 110, MILWAUKEE 91 (37-38)

Small forward Dennis Scott scored a career-high 41 points – including a team-record 9 3-point field goals – to lead the Magic past the Bucks. The victory moved the Magic into a three-way tie with Indiana and Detroit for the final playoff position in the Eastern Conference. All three teams had seven games remaining. Orlando avenged the previous week's loss in Milwaukee, but it was dampened by an injury to starting guard Nick Anderson who left the game in the

second quarter after straining his right hamstring muscle. Scott, who had been in and out of the lineup the last three months because of injuries to his right leg, found a shooting stroke Magic fans haven't seen since early in the season. He finished one 3-point field goal shy of the NBA record set earlier this season by Miami's Brian Shaw. He hit 9 of 19 3-point attempts and 16 of 31 field goals overall. O'Neal had 15 points and 16 rebounds.

THURSDAY, APRIL 15
PHILADELPHIA 101, ORLANDO 95 (37-39)

The Magic came to Philadelphia, but they left their game at home. In the thick of a playoff chase the Magic were drilled by the 76ers. With just six games remaining, Orlando fell a game behind Detroit and Indiana, who shared the eighth Eastern Conference playoff position. The Sixers used the outside-inside combination of guard Jeff Hornacek and rookie forward Clarence Weatherspoon to humble the Magic. Orlando was led by O'Neal, who had 21

points and 11 rebounds, but he also had 4 turnovers.

FRIDAY, APRIL 16
CLEVELAND 113, ORLANDO 110 (37-40)

The Magic finally found that sense of urgency needed for an NBA playoff chase. But they found it a little too late. Despite a furious fourth-quarter rally, the Magic lost to the Cavaliers, falling two games behind Indiana for the last playoff position. The Magic also trailed Detroit. Orlando was behind by 21 points in the third quarter and 14 points midway through the fourth before trimming the deficit to 110-109 with 1:42 remaining. They rallied despite having O'Neal on the bench with five fouls. Scott Skiles had a season-high 21 assists. O'Neal had 24 points and 18 rebounds.

SUNDAY, APRIL 18
ORLANDO 88, BOSTON 79 (38-40)

An ugly finish never felt so fine to the Magic. Desperate for a victory to keep their fading playoff hopes alive,

SITTING (L-R): Jerry Reynolds #35, Dennis Scott #3, Nick Anderson #25, Chris Corchiani #13, Scott Skiles #4, Litterial Green #11, Donald Royal #5, Anthony Bowie #14; STANDING (L-R): Assistant Coach Brian Hill, Director of Player Personnel John Gabriel, COO / General Manager Pat Williams, Head Coach Matt Guokas, Greg Kite #34, Brian Williams #8, Shaquille O'Neal #32, Jeff Turner #31, Terry Catledge #33, Vice-President of Basketball Operations Bob Vander Weide, Strength and Conditioning Coach David Oliver, Video Scout Tom Sterner, Trainer Lenny Currier

they responded with a down-and-dirty defensive effort to stop the Celtics at Orlando Arena. The victory allowed the Magic to draw into a tie with Detroit for ninth place in the Eastern Conference, but it still left them two games out of the final playoff spot. Indiana and Atlanta (40-38) were tied for seventh. All four teams had four games remaining, with the Magic closing the season at home against Atlanta. "At the end, they just add up the wins and losses. They don't ask you how you got them," Magic forward Tom Tolbert said. "It was ugly all right, but we dug down and got it. Maybe the finish belonged in the Hall of Shame, but we had to have it, and we got it." O'Neal scored 20 points and pulled down 21 rebounds – his sixth 20-20 game this season. It was the fewest points ever scored against the Magic.

TUESDAY, APRIL 20
ORLANDO 105, WASHINGTON 86 (39-40)

The Magic cleared the second hurdle of their final-week, uphill quest for the NBA playoffs by drilling the undermanned Bullets at Orlando Arena. They pulled one game behind Indiana for the final Eastern Conference playoff spot. Orlando led from the start, riding O'Neal's superior strength inside to a night filled with easy, fast-break baskets and wide-open jumpers from all angles. O'Neal dominated with 20 points and a team-record 25 rebounds. Nick Anderson led all players with 30 points.

WEDNESDAY, APRIL 21
BOSTON 126, ORLANDO 98 (39-41)

Boston's playoff hopes were now secure, but the same couldn't be said about the Magic's. Despite an awful performance, Orlando remained one game behind the Indiana Pacers in the race for the final Eastern Conference playoff spot. Both teams had two games left. The Magic needed two victories, two Indiana losses and at least one loss by Detroit (which had three games remaining) to reach the playoffs. The Magic rebounded poorly, played defense even worse and failed to protect the basketball. They got 20 points and 10 rebounds from O'Neal and 20 points – including 3 3-pointers – from

point guard Scott Skiles. Little else went right.

FRIDAY, APRIL 23
ORLANDO 119, NEW JERSEY 116 (40-41)

Nick Anderson sat out the first quarter, but he stepped up in the next three, scoring a franchise-record 50 points to keep the Magic's flickering playoff hopes alive. Anderson, who didn't start because of a strained right hamstring muscle, led the Magic to a come-from-behind victory over the Nets. Anderson scored 20 points in the second quarter, 16 in the third and 14 in the fourth. His biggest basket, a short jump shot with 37 seconds remaining, was the winner. The Magic rallied late. Jeff Turner tied the score at 113 with a 3-point basket at 1:07. After O'Neal blocked a shot by Drazen Petrovic on the Nets' next possession, Anderson scored for the lead. He hit 17 of 25 shots from the field and 12 of 12 from the free-throw line. His previous high was 42 points against Miami. "To do this, in this situation, means a lot. The leg was hurting, but I wasn't paying attention to it. If I had to, I was going to drag my leg out there and give it a try." The Magic did it without a big offensive game from O'Neal, who had just 10 points and a season-low 5 rebounds. However, he received the game's biggest ovation late in the first quarter when he broke another goal standard on a thunderous dunk. "It really came crashing down," he said. "It hurt a little bit, but not that much. I have a hard head. It could have been serious, but it wasn't." To secure the final Eastern Conference playoff berth the Magic would have to beat Atlanta at home and hope that Indiana would lose at home to Miami in their final regular-season games.

SATURDAY, APRIL 24
ORLANDO 104, ATLANTA 85 (41-41)

The season didn't end at Orlando Arena. It ended a thousand miles away in Indianapolis, where the Pacers held on to beat the Miami Heat, effectively denying the last playoff spot to Orlando. The Magic did their part, drilling the Hawks in their regular-season finale, but it was the Pacers, who also finished at

41-41, who beat them where it counted most. It took four levels of the NBA's tiebreakers before the Pacers got the nod on point differential in head-to-head matchups – a mere 5 points. "It's disappointing that we didn't reach the playoffs," Coach Guokas said. "But I don't feel like the season was a disappointment." The Magic took care of their business, riding a 31-point, 18-rebound effort from O'Neal. "Our goal this season was to reach .500 or go above, and we accomplished that," Guokas said. "I think you still have to call us a playoff-caliber team. We had a rough final third of the season, but we finally made it back to .500." O'Neal closed his celebrated rookie season much as he started it – with a big game. "I'll see you next season," he said, after watching the Pacers close out the Magic. "Our team did what we had to do tonight, and we got a win. I thought I played well. But it's disappointing not to make the playoffs."

Shaquille O'Neal:

Magic individual season records
Points: 1,893
Blocks: 286
Field goals percentage: .562
Rebounds: 1,122
Field goals made: 733
Personal fouls: 321
Highest scoring average: 23.4 ppg
Disqualifications: 8
Free throws attempted: 721
Free throws made: 427
Turnovers: 307

Magic career records
Blocks: 286

Magic rookie records
(In addition to team records)
Assists: 152
Minutes: 3,071
Games started: 81
Field goal attempts: 1,304

Magic individual game records
Blocked shots: 9 vs. New York (2/14/93)
Rebounds: 25 vs. Washington (4/20/93)
  Defensive: 18 vs. Washington (4/20/93)
Turnovers (tied): 9 vs. Philadelphia (1/18/93)
Field goals made: 19 vs. Detroit (2/16/93)

On growing up

I used to do some crazy stuff when I was a kid, but my father straightened me out. He told me my problem was that I was a follower instead of a leader. Once I established a leadership role, I straightened up. I've been a man since 16.

On drugs

I've got a great life right now, and I'm not going to do anything to mess it up . . . in school they showed you what drugs do to your brain. Drugs are out of the question.

On pressure

Pressure is when you don't know where your next meal is coming from.

On the NBA

It sure is a lot different from the Southeastern Conference where they'd throw ice at you. They'd dump beer on you. They curse you. Man, this is another world.

On money

No one needs as much money as I make.

On laziness

I want to get better every year, every month, every game. I'm paid too much money to sit back and get lazy. That's not me.

On aspiring to greatness

I can't be great every night, but I can try . . . I don't want to play backup to anyone, in anything. I'm not at the top yet, but I will be.

On fans

People read about a superstar and they want to see what he can do. If I was a fan, I'd want to see Shaq, too.

On the media

They can build you up . . . they can bring you down. It's scary.

On autograph-seekers

No more than one item per person.

On wearing wigs to avoid autograph-seekers

When you're 7-1 and you have a jacket with S-H-A-Q on the back, it's hard to be incognito.

On getting away from crowds

I get in my car, turn up the rap music real loud and drive around.

On why Reebok over Nike?

Reebok gave me the opportunity to be The Man. I didn't want to be No. 5 on Nike's list.

On his success

I've been blessed. I wake up every morning and thank God this is my life. I'm so fortunate, sometimes I just can't believe it.

On hitting THE WALL

Hit the wall? If you're coming to ask me if I hit the wall, I haven't. I've never been too tired. If I am, I'll just go get a B12 shot. Take some Vitamin A. Eat a salad. I'm 20, not 30. I have young lungs, young legs.

On the best in the business

Michael Jordan is the best player in the world. That's pretty obvious.

On being like Mike

I someday want to be like Michael Jordan where I can go into any arena in the country and not hear any boos.

On inheriting the legacy of Michael Jordan

Maybe someday I'll be the greatest player in the world. It would be nice to say – someday. Whatever happens happens.

PHOTO CREDITS

Tom Spitz *(The Orlando Sentinel):* ii, 11, 13, 14, 15, 16, 17, 23, 29, 38, 46-47, 49

Michael Meister *(The Arizona Republic):* iii-iv

Basketball Hall of Fame: iv

Mindy Schauer *(The Orlando Sentinel):* v-vi, 19, 28, 31, 46, 54-55, 77

Gary Bogdon *(The Orlando Sentinel):* cover, vii, 2, 3, 6, 7, 13, 18, 19, 20-21, 22, 24-25, 26, 27, 28, 30, 31, 33, 34, 35, 36, 39, 40, 41, 44, 45, 52, 53, 54, 55, 57, 58-59, 60, 61, 62, 63, 64-65, 66, 67, 68-69, 70, 72-73, 75, 82, 84, 85, 86, 87, 91

Phelan Ebenhack *(The Orlando Sentinel):* vii, 6, 25, 33, 37, 50, 71, 74, 81, back cover, softbound edition

Cole High School, San Antonio, Tex.: 2, 4

John Boss *(The Morning Advocate,* Baton Rouge, La.*):* 8

Brad Massina, *Louisiana State University Sports Information Office:* 9

Michael Hults *(The Morning Advocate,* Baton Rouge, La.*):* 9

Joe Burbank *(The Orlando Sentinel):* 12, 13, 52

Tom Burton *(The Orlando Sentinel):* 18, 25, 33, 43, 52

Mic Smith *(The Herald,* Rock Hill, S.C.*):* 32

David Cotton *(The Orlando Sentinel):* 37

Reebok: 40, 41

Pepsi: 42

Kenner Products: 42

John Raoux *(The Orlando Sentinel):* 47

Eileen Samelson *(The Orlando Sentinel):* 46

Boardwalk Realty: 50

Associated Press archives: 58, 59

Bill Kostroun *(The Associated Press):* 87

United Press International: 58, 59

Barry Gossage *(Orlando Magic):* 82

GRAPHIC EMBLEMS

Mark Boivin *(The Orlando Sentinel)*

CONTRIBUTORS

Gene Kruckemyer, Barry Cooper, Marcus B. Williams *(basketball trading cards)*, Carolyn McClendon, Layune McMillan

Giving new meaning to the phrase "crashing the boards," he brought basket, backboard and shot clock down in an April 23 game against the New Jersey Nets. Shaquille 2, Backboards 0.

How the 1992 rookies compared

PLAYER	PTS	REBS	FG%	FT%	MIN
Shaquille O'Neal, Orlando	23.4	13.9	.562	.592	37.9
Alonzo Mourning, Charlotte	21.0	10.3	.511	.781	33.9
Christian Laettner, Minnesota	18.2	8.7	.474	.835	34.9
Jimmy Jackson, Dallas	16.3	4.4	.395	.739	33.5
LaPhonso Ellis, Denver	14.7	9.1	.504	.748	33.5
Tom Gugliotta, Washington	14.7	9.6	.426	.644	34.5
Walt Williams, Sacramento	17.0	4.5	.435	.742	28.4
Todd Day, Milwaukee	13.8	4.1	.432	.717	27.2
Clarence Weatherspoon, Philadelphia	15.6	7.2	.469	.713	32.4
Adam Keefe, Atlanta	6.6	5.3	.500	.700	18.9
Robert Horry, Houston	10.1	4.9	.474	.715	29.5